THE BIBLE IN WORLD HISTORY

THE BIBLE IN WORLD HISTORY

HOW HISTORY AND SCRIPTURE INTERSECT

DR. STEPHEN LESTON

BARBOUR
PUBLISHING

Published by Barbour Publishing, Inc., P.O. Box 719, Uhrichsville, Ohio 44683, www.barbourbooks.com

Our mission is to publish and distribute inspirational products offering exceptional value and biblical encouragement to the masses.

Member of the
Evangelical Christian
Publishers Association

Printed in China.

DEDICATION

It is with profound love and gratitude that I dedicate this book to my wife, who is God's perfect gift for me. I love you with all my heart and have had no greater partner and friend in this world than you! I also want to dedicate this work to my mom and dad. They instilled in me a love for the church that showed me God's purposes for the world and a love for history that showed me God's power in the world. Without their influence this work never would have been written.

Table of Contents

THE FIRST BOOK OF MOSES,

CALLED

GENESIS.

common Year of CHRIST, 4004.——Julian Period, 0710.——Cycle of the Sun, 0010
Cycle of the Moon, 0007.——Indiction, 0005.——Creation from Tisri, or

CHAPTER TWO: THE WORLD TAKES SHAPE 41

THE BIBLE IN HISTORY

WHERE ARE WE HEADED?
The Author's Heart behind This Book

The Christian Bible is a book that is grounded in real history. It records the interactions of God with His creation throughout time. He works among countries, kingdoms, leaders, people, rivers, mountains, and valleys. And ultimately, He is moving His creation to the end that He has appointed for it. In that sense, history truly is "His story," as many have said.

So where is history headed? Revelation 19–21 makes it clear: to a glorious time of justice, a life free from pain for the righteous, and a new world where God will establish His kingdom among people. To study the Bible is truly to study history in the grandest sense.

The idea that a sovereign God is moving all history to His appointed end stands in contrast to many secular views of history. For example, some believe that history is cyclical and thus repeats itself. They reason that just as there are seasons in the world that come and go continually, so, too, history must be nothing more than a cycle of repetitions. The logical conclusion to this line of thought is that the moment in which any one person lives is not as important as it might appear, because history is ultimately going nowhere. Others believe that history is on a course of inevitable progress, meaning that things are continually getting better. Even though a particular nation may decline and fall, the overall trajectory of the world is one of continual progress with no end in sight.

> Only a Christian view of history truly addresses the issues that drive mankind, and thus only a Christian worldview can give us what we need to understand the world around us.

Both of these views, however, stand in opposition to the Christian view of history I have just described. Both non-Christian worldviews do not fully address the overall realities of the world in which we live, and thus fall short in helping us understand the world around us. For example, issues such as meaning, purpose, redemption, forgiveness, and change are not fully addressed in these secular worldviews. I would suggest that only a Christian view of history truly addresses the issues that drive mankind, and thus only a Christian worldview can give us what we need to understand the world around us.

A distinctively Christian view of history adheres to six basic beliefs:*

1. The world was created by God (Genesis 1:1). The universe and all it contains did not come into existence through random chance. It was created with an underlying logic and purpose by God. This, then, means that everyone living in the universe is accountable to God because He created everything with His purposes in mind. The creation is not valued over the Creator. Therefore, the world around us will not operate in the manner it was intended  if the Creator is ignored. As the world rejects God, so, too, will it experience the consequences of living outside the order that God established at creation.

2. God is in control of this world and is moving it in the direction that He sees fit (Psalm 2). Though one cannot fully realize how or to what extent each

*James Montgomery Boice, *Foundations of the Christian Faith: A Comprehensible and Readable Theology* (Downers Grove, IL: InterVarsity Press, 1986), 544–51.

moment fits into the overall direction of the world, we know from scripture that the world is headed in a specific direction. God's grand scheme will only make sense when the end for which the world was created is understood. This is the encouraging message of the book of Revelation.

3. God has revealed Himself in the Bible and in creation (Psalm 19; Romans 1:19). God, who made and rules the world, is not removed from His creation but has made Himself known. God is not hiding from the world but is present, and His nature is seen in both creation and the sixty-six books of the Bible—the Holy Scriptures.

4. Though people have rebelled against God's revelation (Romans 1:18), He has made a way of redemption for mankind. God, in His infinite mercy and love, has made a way for those who have rebelled against Him to be saved from the consequences of sin (Romans 3:21–26). When people are redeemed, they enter into a right understanding of God's creation and begin to walk in the purpose for which mankind was ultimately created. It is through the salvation that God has provided in Jesus Christ that a person can begin to walk in a manner that truly makes sense.

5. Not all desire this redemption, and judgment will come to those who continue in their rebellion (2 Thessalonians 1:5–12). Those who have lived in rebellion against God will pay the eternal consequences in hell. The hope that sustains mankind in the face of all the world's injustices is the promise that God will bring justice to the oppressed and that the oppressors will suffer the consequences of their transgressions.

6. All history and creation exist for the glory of God, and both the redemption and the judgment of mankind will bring glory to Him (Romans 9:19–24; 11:36). This is God's world, and God acts for His glory alone.

The entire world exists to declare God's glory and majesty (Psalm 19). If people fail to understand this key point, the world around them will be incomprehensible. God did not create the world so that people might glorify themselves; He created the world so that He would be glorified in all of His creation. Thus, the glory of God is the fundamental operating principle for understanding the world.

The Bible repeatedly affirms this six-point view of history. Perhaps the clearest presentation of the Christian perspective is found in Acts 17:22–31. However, it can also be found in various forms throughout the Bible. The world makes sense only when we understand it through a biblical world-view. If we fail to embrace God's perspective, then we cannot comprehend the world around us; instead, we are left with nagging questions and a hollow, empty feeling about the purpose of life and the meaning of the world. Thus, the purpose of this book is to present an understanding of the world through the lens of scripture.

COMPLEXITIES IN UNDERSTANDING HISTORY

As we seek to understand the Bible in relation to world history, conflicts will emerge. One of the more pressing problems is how to assign correct dates to the events of world history. For example, many different dates have been suggested concerning when the world began, when certain people lived, and when certain wars took place. It would be foolish to think that any one book can definitively answer all the questions about the proper dating of certain events. Instead, those who examine world history must be honest about the assumptions they make as they interpret the events around them, because these assumptions, or presuppositions, guide the ways in which they interpret historical evidence.

With that in mind, I want to outline from the start the presuppositions

I hold in interpreting the world that will inform how I date certain events. These presuppositions will establish a baseline for our understanding of the world:

1.   The Bible is the Word of God and thus reveals truth.

2.   The Bible, as the Word of God, is the binding authority for understanding the world and humanity, sin and salvation, and God and history.

3.   The world came into existence by the direct will and act of God, just as Genesis 1 teaches.

With these presuppositions in place, we will use the Bible as the basis for understanding God, creation, mankind, the problems in the world, and God's solution to these problems. Therefore, our entire interpretation of the world will be based on a literal understanding and interpretation of the Christian scriptures.

This book focuses on events that took place in world history while the events of the Bible unfolded. Even within these parameters, however, it is not always clear when certain events occurred. The point of this book is not to try

to solve every historical issue surrounding the dating of events, but instead to connect the events of world history with the events of the Bible to show how the Bible gives us the clarity necessary to make sense of the world and world history.

THE NATURE OF HISTORY

One of our underlying assumptions is that God is the God of all history—not just "sacred" history, as some would suggest. All too often, it seems, an unnecessary division is made between sacred and secular history (see definitions below), which appears to be driven by a desire to diminish God's role as the sovereign Lord of the universe. This process of driving a wedge between sacred and secular history is called secularization, which Peter Berger defines more specifically as "the process by which sectors of society and culture are removed from the domination of religious institutions and symbols." The eventual result of this process is that belief in God is relegated to nothing more than a "personal belief" that has no standing in public discourse.

In short, secularization promotes the paradigm that God plays no part in the real world. Instead, belief in God is nothing more than a psychological crutch to help individuals deal with things in the world that they do not understand. By creating an artificial division between the history recorded in the Bible and the history of the "real world," the role of God is diminished and a secular worldview begins to dominate. I reject this notion of the world and believe that an honest look at history will show a harmony between sacred and secular history.

Ceiling of an Orthodox church in South Africa

To help us grasp the unity of all human history, and God's hand at work in the details, I like to look at the topic from three distinct perspectives: *sacred*, *secular*, and *redemptive*.

Sacred history covers the history of the world as recorded in the Bible. Primarily, it is concerned with the formation of the nation of Israel and the events that led to the establishment of the Christian church. The scope of this history is fairly narrow, in that it covers only specific events as they relate to the two main topics at hand: Israel and the church.

Secular history, as I am using the term, refers to history and events not directly mentioned in scripture. In this study of history, there is no central focal point (i.e., Israel or the church); instead, the view is general and broad, with the goal of tracking movements of the entire world.

Redemptive history is similar to sacred history in that it covers events described in the Bible. The difference is that redemptive history is chiefly concerned with events that directly connect and relate to the specific plan of salvation that God has designed for the world. In other words, redemptive history focuses on events that directly pertain to the first coming of Jesus Christ, and also to His second coming, which has yet to occur.

In studying history, there are moments when all three perspectives converge in a single event, and there we can see the hand of God at work. In my personal study of history, I have observed how the events of secular history have had an impact on sacred history, and vice versa. This reciprocal impact is most evident when secular and sacred events coalesce to bring about God's plan for redemptive history.

As we study the fullness of history unfolding before us, we can see God at work in the world, carrying out His plan for the ages. It is then that the study of history becomes more than a survey of past events and instead begins to uncover the work and purposes of God. This is when history becomes very real to us and builds our faith as we live in the time and place of history in which God has placed us.

In the pages to follow, we will survey some of the major movements in world history. These movements, far from a random collection of events, are movements directed by God, leading to a very important work for Israel and the world. If we merely look at the world through the lens of secular history, we will see only power shifts—one nation rising up as another declines. Yet if we add to our understanding of secular history both sacred and redemptive perspectives, we will see that the world is not just moving through a series of random or repetitive cycles but toward the establishment of God's eternal kingdom with God's King—Jesus Christ—ruling on its throne.

> The events of the world are not separate from the events recorded in scripture.

With this in mind, let us now turn our attention to the Bible, and we will see that the events of the world are not separate from the events recorded in scripture. As we come to recognize this truth, we will be able to better understand the Bible, the world, and the very heart of God.

CHAPTER 1

FROM CREATION TO THE TOWER OF BABEL

THE BEGINNING

The story of the Bible begins in a part of the world that is rich with life, tradition, history, and human culture. It is a place in which the world as we know it was formed and shaped. But before we make our way to the very beginning of time, we must first stop at the year 2066 BC and look at a man named Abram.

Abram lived in a place called Ur, which is in modern-day Iraq. He was a very important figure in Old Testament history because he was called by God to leave his homeland and settle in a new and unfamiliar place. This place was far from his home of origin, and he would not be welcomed there. Instead, he would be regarded as a threat. Yet through this man's obedience,

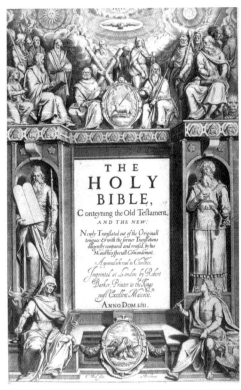

Front page to the King James Version, 1611, shows the twelve apostles at the top. Moses and Aaron flank the central text. In the four corners sit Matthew, Mark, Luke, and John, with their symbolic animals. At the top is the Holy Spirit in the form of a dove.

a nation was formed that would become the center of biblical history and a focal point of the world today: Israel.

Abram rejected the polytheistic views of his day and of his fellow countrymen.

During Abram's time, Ur was a leading city. The religious worldview of the city—and of the Near Eastern world in general—was that a universal sea was the source of all creation. This primeval sea gave birth to the mountains, which united heaven and earth. The gods were not the makers of the sea but actually came from this sea. These gods had human characteristics: some were male and some female. They had emotions, were capable of both love and hate, and could act in both rational and irrational manners. Many believed that the gods eventually united together and produced the rest of creation, including other gods that ruled over smaller parts of creation.

The people of ancient Ur believed that the universe was ruled by these various gods, whose power was seen through natural phenomena such as rainfall, the cycle of planting and harvesting, and the circuit of the sun and phases of the moon. Each city in this part of the world had its own deity to whom the citizens paid homage. Temples, known as ziggurats, were often constructed to honor their city's god. Religion and idol worship played a major role in community life, and priests held positions of honor in society.

Abram rejected the polytheistic views of his day and of his fellow countrymen. Instead, he believed in one creator God who ruled the earth and directed the world toward His own final outcome. When God called Abram to leave his home to settle in a new land (Genesis 12), Abram did so with the understanding that the God who called him was the God of all creation. He knew that this was the one true God and that he was to give his full allegiance to Him all the days of his life.

Abraham's servant swears to his master, as in Genesis 24:9: "And the servant put his hand under the thigh of Abraham his master, and sware to him concerning that matter" (KJV). Illustration from the 1728 *Figures de la Bible*, illustrated by Gerard Hoet (1648–1733) and others, and published by P. de Hondt in The Hague.

But what would it mean for Abram to hold to this view? What are the theological ramifications of giving sole allegiance to one God who rules heaven and earth? What was it that drove Abram away from his homeland and all the potential wealth that it held for him? Why become a sojourner and face the trials that such a life would bring? To understand Abram and his decision, we must look at the start of it all; we must draw our attention to the beginning of the Bible to discover the foundation of Abram's hope.

THE START OF IT ALL: CREATION

Abram believed in one God, called Yahweh—not a multiplicity of gods—and Yahweh was not only the ruler of the world but its creator as well. This revelation is given to mankind in the first chapter of the book of Genesis. But to learn this truth, Abram would not have turned to the first chapter of the Bible like we would today.

The book of Genesis was not written until long after the time of

"In the beginning God created the heavens and the earth" (Genesis 1:1).

Abram—six hundred years or more. So how would Abram have known the story of creation and the reality of the existence of God? And how was Moses able to write about something that happened so many years before he was born?

For several of the accounts in Genesis, there is much evidence that Moses had access to material that had already been recorded by others. In other words, Moses was not the first person to write a history of the world—he was just the first to do so under the inspiration of the Holy Spirit (see 2 Timothy 3:16; 2 Peter 1:21). It was under the inspiration of the Holy Spirit that Moses

Moses was the first person to write a history of the world under the inspiration of the Holy Spirit. In this photograph, a Hebrew scribe meticulously copies the Hebrew Scriptures by hand. This tradition has been done with painstaking accuracy for thousands of years.

collected these accounts and recorded them in Genesis. Evidence for Moses' use of previously recorded material can be found in eleven occurrences in Genesis of lists given of the generations of a particular person (2:4; 5:1; 6:9; 10:1; 11:10; 11:27; 25:12; 25:19; 36:1; 36:9; 37:2). Each list is a collection of information that resembles the way a family would record their personal heritage. It is easy to see how Moses could have taken other written accounts and compiled them under the inspiration of the Holy Spirit. This does not mean that God did not reveal other unique information to Moses along the way. However, it does suggest that some historical records of events had already

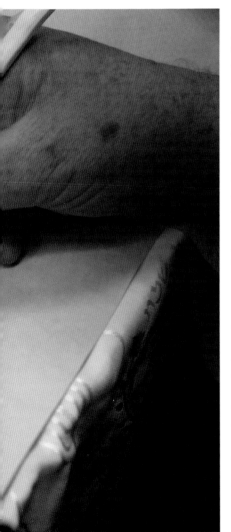

been written or passed down by oral tradition and it was through the Holy Spirit that Moses was able to discern which accounts were true and include them, and also to filter out the accounts that were false.

Therefore, it is not unreasonable to believe that Abram would have had access not only to the historical accounts passed down through oral tradition, but to written accounts as well. Knowing that the Word of God could have been revealed to him directly, as well as through the written accounts passed down from the beginning of history, we can easily see how Abram could have gained an understanding of the existence and rule of God. Hebrews 1:1 makes it clear that God speaks, and thus He could have communicated with Abram through various means.

As we seek to understand Abram's mind-set as he moved from his home in Ur to Canaan, we must go back to the beginning of God's revelation—the book of Genesis. It is in Genesis that we are given the foundation for understanding the creation of the world, what went wrong, and the basis for interpreting subsequent world history.

THE BASIS FOR UNDERSTANDING

In Genesis we gain insights into why the world is the way it is and why certain events occurred in the world as they did.

In the first chapter of Genesis, we read about the creation of the world, outlined in the following chart.

VERSE	DAY	DAYS OF FORMING
1:2	1	The substance of the heavens and earth
1:3	1	Light
1:7	2	Separation of waters—sky
1:9–11	3	Dry land—vegetation

VERSE	DAY	DAYS OF FILLING
1:14	4	Light—sun, moon, stars
1:21	5	The fish of the sea and the birds of the air
1:24	6	The animals that walk upon the earth
1:26	6	Mankind

THE KEY TO UNDERSTANDING THE BIBLICAL ACCOUNT OF CREATION IS TO GRASP THAT THE WORLD WAS NOT A PLACE WHERE MAN JUST HAPPENED UPON THE SCENE THROUGH SOME MISTAKE OR RANDOM CHANCE. THE WORLD WAS CREATED BY GOD FOR MAN TO LIVE IN, FOR THE PURPOSE OF GLORIFYING HIM. LIKEWISE, ALL MEN AND WOMEN ON EARTH ARE DESCENDED FROM ONE SINGLE PAIR: ADAM AND EVE.

Because all humanity descended from this one pair, there is no one group that is ultimately favored over another. All are equal, and all have a place and a purpose within creation. The importance of this point is that, as much as people, in their arrogance, want to set one nationality above another, all are

The Garden of Eden has been a favorite setting for artists throughout the ages. On the facing page are classic paintings on the topic. Top left: Thomas Cole, *The Garden of Eden*. Painted in 1828. Top right: *The Earthly Paradise* (Garden of Eden), painted by Hieronymus Bosch in the early sixteenth century as part of *The Garden of Earthly Delights*. Upper center left: Spring by Niccolò Possino. Painted in the early seventeenth century. Upper center: The four rivers and the gates of Paradise. Painted in the twelfth century on parchment. Bottom half: Painting called *Paradise* by Lucas Cranach (1472–1553). Work completed in 1536.

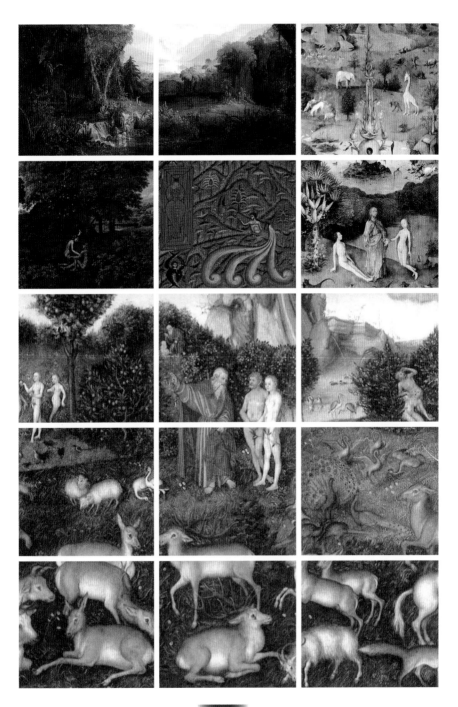

equal. Ultimately, every person in the world is descended from one set of parents, who were created by God; thus we all come from one source—the hand of God. As we look at the first set of parents in the world, we can learn much about the world and the shaping of its history.

ADAM AND EVE

In Genesis 1:26, we learn something very important about the first humans on earth:

■ *Then God said, "Let us make man in our image, after our likeness. And let them have dominion over the fish of the sea and over the birds of the heavens and over the livestock and over all the earth and over every creeping thing that creeps on the earth."*

> **For more details on Creation, read Genesis 1.**

Rather than create mankind with the phrase "Let there be," as God did with all the other things He created, God created humans with the words "Let us make." Thus, even by the very words He used to create people, God fashioned

The Garden of Eden was located between the Tigris and Euphrates Rivers.

them to be different from the rest of creation. Mankind's distinctiveness must be acknowledged and respected.

But what was it exactly that made humanity different from all other creatures? Was it simply the words God used when man was created? No, it was much more than that. The essence of man's uniqueness lies in his having been created in the image of God (1:26). "Created in God's image" means that man has the ability to reflect the character of God. For example:

1. Mankind rules over creation with authority delegated by God (1:26).
2. Mankind was created male and female; in both man and woman, God has chosen to bear His image (1:27).
3. Mankind was commanded to fill the earth, specifically by bearing offspring (1:28). This command calls upon humans to share in the creative process. Humans do not become God, but they have the joy of sharing in the creative process as God brings humanity into being through them.

Keep in mind that the uniqueness of mankind is found in the combination of these characteristics. In other words, animals also procreate, yet they do not share in the ruling over creation and the image-bearing components that make mankind unique. The ability to reflect the image of God in these ways sets mankind apart from the rest of creation and demonstrates that humans hold a unique place in the world. Mankind's distinction is further highlighted in Genesis 1:29–30:

■ *And God said, "Behold, I have given you every plant yielding seed that is on the face of all the earth, and every tree with seed in its fruit. You shall have them for food. And to every beast of the earth and to every bird of the heavens and to everything that creeps on the earth, everything that has the breath of life, I have given every green plant for food." And it was so.*

In this passage, we see that men and women are creatures who are able to think, reason, act, interact, make decisions, create, and fill—all aspects that reflect their Creator. God did this because He planned to interact with His creation in a highly progressive and relational manner. Mankind, as part

Adam and Eve, stained glass window. Original location unknown.

of that creation, would not only interact with God but also be accountable to Him for what they did. God did not create mankind to live merely by instinct, but to have reason and thought and reflection in all that they do on earth. God gave people the ability to work and exist as participants in history.

God also made the earth to provide what mankind needed to survive. God's gift of a world that could sustain mankind, and His command to subdue and interact with it, was given so that humanity would reflect His glory and image in the world (see Colossians 1:15–20; Revelation 4:11).

> In Genesis 3, Adam and Eve rebelled against God, and nothing has been the same ever since.

Genesis 1 seems to give the impression that all should be good and harmonious between mankind and the rest of creation. Yet a quick look at the rest of scripture—and at the world as we know it—makes it clear that such is not the case. So what happened? Sin entered the world. In Genesis 3, Adam and Eve rebelled against God, and nothing has been the same ever since.

Not only did this rebellion mar Adam and Eve directly, but it also meant that sin entered all that came from Adam and Eve. Therefore, every human being since Adam and Eve (with the sole exception of Jesus Christ) has been born into sin. This sin is what introduced war, adultery, betrayal, espionage, pain, and misery into the world and into the lives of every human being.

The sin that Adam and Eve committed was based on a mistaken belief that they could live their lives independently of God and His rule. At this point, humanity began to attempt to usurp the role of God and act like gods themselves. Hence, history took a turn. Rather than live in harmony with God and all creation, mankind would now live in conflict with both.

Such discord can be seen in the rise and fall of nations throughout history. All have followed the same trajectory: a rise to power, a consolidation of power, an abuse of power, and a fall from power. The demise of nations stems from the very same root as the fall of Adam and Eve: a false belief that mankind can rise to ultimate power. In other words, embedded in the sin nature of humanity is a desire to rule the world. This is the message of Psalm 2. Warfare is a perpetual part of human history because everyone wants to fill the position reserved for Jesus Christ— that is, King of kings. That's why human history often seems like nothing

more than the study of conflict and war. The Bible gives us an understanding of history that helps make sense of our troubled world.

The Bible has more to say about the world around us than just what we learn from Adam and Eve. When we look at the children of Adam and Eve, we get an understanding of how the human sin nature manifests itself in the lives of individual people.

Statue of Cain and Abel at cathedral in Milan, Italy.

CAIN AND ABEL

Cain, the first son of Adam and Eve, was born after the Fall (the sin of Adam and Eve in the Garden of Eden). Abel was born next. We do not know if others were born shortly after these two, but given the way the narrative plays out, it is safe to assume that this was the case.

Cain and Abel both brought offerings to the Lord. Abel's was accepted and Cain's was rejected. Many have wondered why the two men were suddenly making offerings to the Lord when nothing had been mentioned yet about the need for offerings. However, Moses' goal, in recording early human history, was not to write an exhaustive account but instead to hit the high points that we need to understand in order for the world to make sense. We can infer that Adam and Eve understood that they had sinned against God (they clearly experienced the consequences of their sin), so it is reasonable to assume that they understood that some type of offering would be needed as appeasement for their sin.

In any case, the text suggests that as Cain and Abel brought their offerings, they were also seeking God's acceptance. However, Cain's offering was rejected, and this posed a problem for him. Rather than seeking to do what was right and bring a proper offering to the Lord, Cain chose

Cain and Abel, ivory panel from the Cathedral of Salerno, ca. AD 1084

instead to kill his brother. The jealousy in his heart was greater than his desire to be right with God. Thus, in this moment, we see the true depth of human depravity. A man is killed by his brother, not for anything he did, but because the murderer was not right with God and was therefore filled with hate. Cain acted in a way that ignored God and treated God's way, word, and path for forgiveness as worthless.

This act of murder gives us some important insights into the ways of the world. We see in the killing of Abel that the heart of man is truly wicked. When this wickedness goes unchecked, the result is murder. This explains why the study of history inevitably exposes us to brutality. This brutality is not just in the heart of Cain; it exists in the hearts of all those who live in rebellion against God. Cain quickly became afraid of the consequences of his sin, because the world around him was filled with sinners who were equally depraved as he was. Cain saw that just as his sin had led him to murder, others too were capable of murder (Genesis 4). God sentenced Cain to wander the earth as a nomad; and because the people in the world at that time disdained wanderers, Cain was afraid. What would this world have been like?

> Rather than seeking to do what was right and bring a proper offering to the Lord, Cain chose instead to kill his brother. The jealousy in his heart was greater than his desire to be right with God.

Before we can understand the world of Cain, we must first address a very important question: How did the world become populated so quickly that Cain would have been afraid to be sent into exile? In other words, where did all these people come from whom Cain feared?

In order to answer this, we must first keep in mind that we do not know at what age Cain killed Abel. The first eleven chapters of Genesis cover about two thousand years of history in a rather quick manner. Therefore, Cain and Abel could well have been between the ages of fifty and one hundred when this sin occurred. This is important to note, because the older they were, the longer the earth would have had to become populated.

For more details on Cain and Abel, read Genesis 4.

Leon Morris observes in Genesis 5 that each patriarch lived many hundreds of years and fathered sons and daughters. From this he concludes that if each man fathered six children—three sons and three daughters—and each of these children grew to maturity, married, and continued the same trend, the earth's population would have grown to at least 120,000 people within the first 800 years—a span of years likely within Cain's lifetime. This hypothetical equation shows that it is not unreasonable to believe that Cain would have been afraid of being mistreated once he left his home. At the time of Abel's murder, he and Cain were not the only people on earth besides Adam and Eve.

TECHNOLOGICAL ADVANCEMENT

As Cain went out into exile, what was the world like? Archaeologists have shed some rather fascinating light on the time from Cain to the Flood.

Besides being well populated by the time of Abel's murder, the world was also a place of incredible technological advancement. Genesis 4 notes the advancements of three of Cain's descendants: Jabal, "the father of those who dwell in tents and have livestock"; Jubal, "the father of all those who play the lyre and pipe"; and Tubal-cain, "the forger of all instruments of bronze and iron" (Genesis 4:20–22).

From these brief descriptions, we can see that, from the beginning, God fashioned within mankind the ability to use God's creation for the purpose of survival and enjoyment. The technological advancements made during the time of Cain rivaled those of the nineteenth and twentieth centuries of the modern era. Through the descendants of Adam and Eve, God filled the earth with people who had the creativity, skill, and ability to subdue the earth and rule it.

During this time, the world witnessed the invention of the wheel, sailing ships, metallurgy, and oven-baked pottery. These inventions were developed in the area called Mesopotamia, the region where the first inhabitants of the earth lived. According to archaeological records, this area was one of the first regions settled in history. This supports the theory that the Garden of Eden was located in this area.

According to Genesis 2:14, the Tigris and the Euphrates flowed through Eden. Thus, when Adam and Eve were expelled from the garden, they most likely settled somewhere in the vicinity of these two rivers. The fertile area between the Tigris and Euphrates formed a very important area of development for the ancient world. Along these rivers, a series of cities emerged that Cain would certainly have had contact with in his travels.

This region is known as the Fertile Crescent, due to its shape and the fertility of its land. The Fertile Crescent is regarded as the birthplace of civilization. It was also here that the first written language was developed—cuneiform, a script written on clay tablets. Other developments include the plow and the first-known use of hours and minutes to measure time.

What was life like for those who lived in the Fertile Crescent? How technologically sophisticated would they have been?

Agriculture

The main means of survival during this time was agriculture. In the Fertile Crescent, archaeologists have uncovered early forms of irrigation and many types of farming implements. As noted earlier, the first wheel was developed

THE NEAR EAST DURING
THE TIME OF THE PATRIARCHS

→ Abram travels from Ur to Haran

→ Abram travels from Haran to Canaan

→ Abram travels from Canaan to Egypt

Copyright © 2007 by Barbour Publishing, Inc.

in this area. Early forms of conveyance utilized logs as rollers for carts, so that the cart would move much like a modern conveyor belt. Over time, the use of logs evolved into the development of axles and wheels as we know them today.

The Sumerians, the earliest civilization to develop in this region, grew many kinds of crops, including barley, chickpeas, lentils, millet, wheat, turnips, dates, onions, garlic, lettuce, leeks, and mustard. The Sumerians also raised cattle, sheep, goats, and pigs. They used oxen as their primary beasts of burden and donkeys as their primary transport animals. They were also hunters and fishermen. Sumerian agriculture depended heavily on irrigation. The irrigation was accomplished by the use of canals, channels, dikes, weirs, and reservoirs. In short, their world was highly developed, and their way of life was advanced.

International Trade

Technological development was accompanied by economic development. Discoveries of ancient records show the existence of a trade network that ranged from modern-day Afghanistan to Bahrain in the Persian Gulf. Wood, beads, inventions, and other usable goods were traded among the various cities. This trade added to the economic stability of the land and the overall prosperity of the people.

Written Language

The development of writing was one of the more important advancements of early Sumerian culture. Though written artifacts have been discovered in many ancient cultures and in numerous locations throughout the world, the

Assyrian cuneiform script. Though this engraving was created ca. 865–860 BC, it highlights the culture's early interest in both agriculture and the written language.

Sumerians are credited with developing the earliest-known form of writing, which appeared around 3500 BC. Clay tablets from this era were unearthed by archaeologists at Tell Asmar in Iraq.

These tablets contain simple pictures that represent objects or thoughts. The Sumerians eventually simplified their pictures into a series of wedge-shaped signs that were pressed into clay. This is what is known today as cuneiform.

The invention of writing provided a major revolution for the world—it sparked the dawn of the information age. Writing allowed news to be spread, records to be kept, and important events to be memorialized. Based on the examples of writing that have been found, it appears that writing was developed first as a record-keeping tool for business transactions. Over time, cuneiform also came to be used to create educational material and works of literature.

One of the oldest-known written stories, the *Epic of Gilgamesh*, also came from the region of the Fertile Crescent. This story about the king of Uruk

Bill of sale of a male slave and a building in Shuruppak. Sumerian clay tablet, ca. 2600 BC.

(probably biblical Erech) did not emerge until more than a thousand years after writing had been developed. Nevertheless, this story is filled with a lot of important information about life in ancient Mesopotamia. Though it is not part of the Bible and is not consistent with Hebrew and Christian beliefs, it does make allusions to characters, places, and events that are also mentioned in scripture, such as the Garden of Eden and characters that resemble Adam and Eve. This confirms that the Bible records historical events that other ancient sources acknowledge.

Religious Development

In order to better understand the religious developments of the world, it is helpful to ask why religion ever developed at all. In other words, what drove mankind to seek the transcendent? There is a somewhat obscure passage of the Bible that might help us:

Izdubar strangling a lion. Illustration for an 1876 printing of the *Epic of Gilgamesh.*

■ *Lamech said to his wives: "Adah and Zillah, hear my voice; you wives of Lamech, listen to what I say: I have killed a man for wounding me, a young man for striking me. If Cain's revenge is sevenfold, then Lamech's is seventy-sevenfold"* (*Genesis 4:23–24*).

Lamech's declaration appears to typify the culture of his time, showing it to be ruthless and cruel. This is also confirmed by the many wars that ravaged the earth during this time. This leaves us with the sense that things were not right in the world, so mankind sought to transcend its own depravity and reach for something greater and more glorious, some form of divine presence in the world.

Man sees the divine reflection of God in creation; but because of his rebellion, he fails to look to the source of the reflection and instead worships the creation (Romans 1:18–23). Thus, humanity reached out for spirituality, rather than to the Creator, and this gave rise to the many religions of the ancient world. From archaeological digs in the Fertile Crescent, it has become clear that religion played a major role in the region.

IT IS INTERESTING TO NOTE THAT VIRTUALLY EVERYONE IN THE WORLD AT THIS TIME WORSHIPPED SOMETHING. THERE ARE NO KNOWN GROUPS THAT DID NOT BELIEVE IN ANY GODS AT ALL. THE ONLY DIFFERENCES WERE IN WHAT AND HOW THEY WORSHIPPED. WORSHIP PLAYED A CENTRAL ROLE IN ANCIENT LIFE. FOR THIS REASON, IF SOMEONE DID NOT PRACTICE THE SAME WORSHIP AS OTHERS IN THE SAME AREA, THAT PERSON WOULD BE UNABLE TO PARTICIPATE IN BUSINESS, ENTERTAINMENT, OR POLITICAL LIFE. THUS, CAIN WOULD HAVE FOUND HIMSELF AS AN OUTCAST IN THE WORLD.

Man sees the divine reflection of God in creation; but because of his rebellion, he fails to look to the source of the reflection and instead worships the creation (Romans 1:18–23).

War and Conflict

As the world developed, it also increased in violence. As regions were established, conflicts inevitably began to surface, motivated by the desire for power and control. As cities vied for power, wars became common. Tribalism fueled suspicion and dislike between differing cultural groups. Thus, a person from one city might not be accepted in another city. The time of war and conflict reached its apex during the days of Noah.

THE AGE OF NOAH

In Genesis 6:5, we see just how bad things had become in the world:

■ *The L*ORD *saw that the wickedness of man was great in the earth, and that every intention of the thoughts of his heart was only evil continually.*

For more details on the Flood, read Genesis 6–9.

By Noah's time, wickedness ruled the world. Mankind had become evil to such a degree that God was grieved that He had even made people (Genesis 6:6). To have "every intention" of their thoughts and hearts be evil means that the people had reached the point where they would rebel against God's plan for humanity without question.

From remains discovered from this time period (roughly 2300 BC), a rather gruesome picture emerges. As archaeologists have unearthed bodies of people who lived in Mesopotamia, they have found evidence that cannibalism was practiced. In short, this was a very brutal era, in which humanity showed little to no regard for one another. This may be what God meant when He

observed the wickedness of the people and was grieved for His creation.

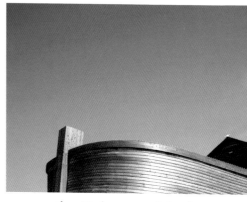

In January 1996 National Geographic did a comparison between rodeo riders and their injuries, and skeletons uncovered from the time of Noah. They found striking similarities between the injuries of the two groups, suggesting that this was a very violent society. When people reject God and the boundaries and purposes that He has created for them, they become a law unto themselves, and society becomes weaker and more dangerous. The net result is always extreme anarchy and a violent world.

Because of the extreme evil in the world, God flooded the earth. In essence, He chose to start over. God knew that the world that would form after the Flood would not be a world without evil, but that it would be a world in which a fixed set of laws would be enacted for all humanity. After Noah and his family left the ark, God fixed His law upon the hearts of mankind.

■ *And God blessed Noah and his sons and said to them, "Be fruitful and multiply and fill the earth. The fear of you and the dread of you shall be upon every beast of the earth and upon every bird of the heavens, upon everything that creeps on the ground and all the fish of the sea. Into your hand they are delivered. Every moving thing that lives shall be food for you. And as I gave you the green plants, I give you everything. But you shall not eat flesh with its life, that is, its blood. And for your lifeblood I will require a reckoning: from every beast I will require it and from man. From his fellow man I will require a reckoning for the life of man.*

Whoever sheds the blood of man, by man shall his blood be shed, for God made man in his own image. And you, be fruitful and multiply, teem on the earth and multiply in it" (Genesis 9:1–7).

After the Flood, God established a set of laws that directed people to regard human life with dignity. This was an important development, because it allowed for the formalization of social laws designed to protect people and avert anarchy. God instituted an advancement of social order that would enable a society to survive. This had a great impact on the development of governmental systems and allowed society to advance in ways it had not advanced before the Flood. After the Flood, we also see the emergence of one of the first powerful leaders in world history.

(Left) Bronze head of a king, most likely Sargon of Akkad but possibly Naram-Sin. Unearthed in Nineveh (now in Iraq).

SARGON OF AKKAD

Sargon of Akkad started life in a humble manner, having been adopted by a gardener as a child. He eventually rose to a position of power and conquered all the great kings around him, creating an empire that united all of Mesopotamia. He reigned for fifty-five years (2270–2215 BC). Sargon reigned over one of the first massive empires and ushered in a season of intense conflict in the Mesopotamian world. He is considered the first military dictator, and his army is believed to have been the first full-time regular army in the world.

THE FOLLOWING ARE SOME OF THE ACCOMPLISHMENTS THAT WERE MADE THROUGH SARGON'S REIGN:
- THE FIRST GOVERNMENT BUREAUCRACY
- THE STANDARDIZATION OF WEIGHTS AND MEASUREMENTS
- A NATIONAL TAX SYSTEM MANAGED BY GOVERNMENT OFFICIALS TO PAY FOR THE MILITARY AND OTHER MEMBERS OF THE KING'S STAFF

Under the rule of Sargon, the concept of national power was realized for the first time. This advancement led people to model their future governments after Sargon's system. This combined power of people is not always a good thing—especially when that power is used to try to thwart God's purposes. Similarly, the Bible records another incident in which people unified for the purpose of making a name for themselves.

THE DAY THE WORLD CHANGED

Genesis 11 records the building of an extraordinary structure that is often referred to as the Tower of Babel. The construction of this tower literally changed the world.

For more details on Babel, read Genesis 11.

What makes this story unique is that this tower was more than just the expression of a pagan religious tradition. Instead, it showed how powerful the collected rebellion of mankind could be when every human was able to communicate without hindrance. Unity of speech fostered advancements rivaled only by those in our own day and age. However, this unfettered ability to advance had to be stopped, for if it was used to rebel against God, judgment would inevitably follow. Thus God, in His mercy, sought to slow down mankind's ability to communicate in order to provide more time for God's plan of redemption to be carried out.

The City of Man Formed

The critical backdrop for the story of the Tower of Babel is set in the first two verses of Genesis 11:

■ *Now the whole earth had one language and the same words. And as people migrated from the east, they found a plain in the land of Shinar and settled there.*

Immediately after the Flood, people returned to the Fertile Crescent (the land of Shinar). This fertile and productive region was quickly developed and heavily fought over.

One of mankind's early developments was the ability to design and make buildings. As part of God's command for mankind to subdue the earth, He gave humanity all the faculties necessary to design and create great structures. Yet, in man's rebellion, these structures were created to rebel against God and not to honor and glorify Him.

■ *And they said to one another, "Come, let us make bricks, and burn them thoroughly." And they had brick for stone, and bitumen for mortar. Then they said, "Come, let us build ourselves a city and a tower with its top in the heavens, and let us make a name for ourselves, lest we be dispersed over the face of the whole earth"* (Genesis 11:3–4).

With their growing advancement in the ability to work together, mankind made plans to accomplish four key things:

1. Build a city. The people wanted to bring everyone together to form a grand city that would exceed the

Left: Woodcut from early English Bible. Original artist and date unknown.

Right: German print named *God Watching the Tower of Babel*. Original artist and date unknown.

glory of all other cities. They sought to unify the world around this vision.

2. Build a tower. This tower was to have "its top in the heavens." In Hebrew, the phrase "with its top in the heavens" can mean various things. The first is that the tower literally was intended to reach heaven. It could also mean that the tower was dedicated to the heavens. The third is that the tower was simply going to be very tall. The last two meanings are most likely intended here; this was a tall structure that was dedicated to the heavens. All towers built at this time were dedicated to some religious function, but this one seems to have been different in its size and scope. This tower was built to allow someone to rule from the heavens, thereby demonstrating his great power as well as intimidating those around him.

3. Make a name for themselves. To *make a name for* themselves literally means to bring glory to themselves. They designed a city and a religion

The construction of ziggurats occurred throughout the ancient world. Their similarities in design point to the common ancestry of all peoples. The top two ziggurats were built in Central America, while the one on the bottom was built in the ancient city of Ur (in modern-day Iraq).

around the glory of man. All humanistic religions share in one single motivation: to be man-centered and man-honoring. The people wanted to exert their glory over both God and the world.

4.   Prevent being dispersed. At this point, the area of the world experiencing the greatest development was the Fertile Crescent. The people congregated in this area, and their temple was the building that they developed to mark their presence there.

What was this temple like? In ancient Mesopotamia, there was a type of structure called a ziggurat that dates to a time after the Flood. Interestingly, this same type of structure is seen in other parts of the world. It is not unreasonable to believe that the Tower of Babel most likely reflected this shape as well. The reason for this belief is that after God dispersed the people who built the tower, it appears that they took this type of building design with them wherever they went. Look at the similarities of these structures that appear on the facing page.

> All humanistic religions share in one single motivation: to be man-centered and man-honoring. The people wanted to exert their glory over both God and the world.

After this temple was constructed, God responded, and His response completely changed the world for all history.

The City of Man Hindered

■ *And the* LORD *came down to see the city and the tower, which the children of man had built. And the* LORD *said, "Behold, they are one people, and they have all one language, and this is only the beginning of what they will do. And nothing that they propose to do will now be impossible for them"* (Genesis 11:5–6).

The idea here is not that the Lord did not know what was happening up to this point but instead that God had decided the time was right to come to earth to deal with it. The people had completed this tower, which means that God had allowed mankind to have a certain amount of freedom and to use their abilities to a certain point; and now God was going to respond. This passage may have been written in this manner to show us how God interacts

God hindered mankind's ability to work together at an advanced pace.

with humanity. He allows for an interplay between Himself and us, and responds to our actions.

It is important to mark a contrast found in Genesis 11:5. In the preceding verses, we see man building a tower to heaven; then, in verse 5, we see God coming down to look at it. This shows us how high and lofty God is. Moses wanted us to see the tower in relation to God in this passage. As tall as this tower was—"with its top in the heavens"—the one true God still sat above it.

The first thing God did was to observe mankind's potential. Working together, mankind could harness its resources for a lot of evil. In other words, if mankind were able to stay as a unit, to forge all of its abilities into a single project, a lot of evil could come as a result. When the nations of the world unite for war, they become a powerful force. If all unredeemed humanity could communicate without any difficulties, then the forces of evil would become a huge hindrance to the spreading of the gospel.

■ *"Come, let us go down and there confuse their language, so that they may not understand one another's speech" (Genesis 11:7).*

Note the play on words in Genesis 11:4–7. The people of the world say, "Come, let us build a one-world religion." Then God comes and says, "Come, let us break them up."

They do not want to be dispersed, yet this is exactly what happened. Besides being dispersed geographically, the people were also now hindered in their ability to communicate. At the heart of this breakup was the introduction of languages, but it also led to the development of different cultures and cultural worldviews. In order to obstruct the development of technology, God hindered mankind's ability to work together at an advanced pace. This allowed God to bring about His plan for a Messiah without first having to bring about another universal judgment to stop the evil.

■ *So the LORD dispersed them from there over the face of all the earth, and they left off building the city (Genesis 11:8).*

At this point, the city is abandoned, because mankind could no longer advance at the rate it had progressed when everyone was able to work together. God allowed people just enough advancement to use what they had been given, but now they were prevented from carrying out as much evil as before. Advancement does not always bring about progress. Advancement left unchecked will always lead to pain, misery, and rebellion. Here God was merciful to stop this from happening.

■ *Therefore its name was called Babel, because there the LORD confused the language of all the earth. And from there the LORD dispersed them over the face of all the earth. (Genesis 11:9).*

GENESIS 11:9 REVEALS WHY THIS PLACE WAS CALLED BABEL. THIS IS ALSO WHY THERE ARE SO MANY NATIONS IN THE WORLD WITH VARIOUS PAGAN RELIGIONS, AND WHY BABYLON IS OFTEN A SYMBOL OF EVIL IN THE SCRIPTURES. GOD CONFUSED THEIR LANGUAGES, STOPPED THE REBELLION, AND SLOWED DOWN THE ADVANCEMENT OF THE CITY THAT WAS BEING DEVELOPED TO GLORIFY MAN INSTEAD OF GOD. IT IS FROM THIS STORY THAT WE CAN TRULY UNDERSTAND WHY THERE ARE MANY DIFFERENT CULTURES IN THE WORLD.

REFLECTIONS

Even though there are some complexities in understanding the world and its history, some things become clear as we look at the world through the lens of scripture. We can see why there is war, where the ideas of justice and self-preservation come from, why the world is divided as it is, and how we have inherited some of the basic advancements we take for granted (e.g., reading, writing, the wheel). The world we live in today began taking shape right from the beginning, and scripture enables us to see the forces at work more clearly.

The world was created by God for His glory (Colossians 1:15–20; Revelation 4:11). When mankind rebels against this purpose, problems come into the world that can only be answered by submitting to the King of kings and Lord of lords, Jesus Christ (Psalm 2). In Christ there is hope, and we must embrace that hope in order to have meaning and purpose in this world.

TIME LINE
CREATION — 2200 BC

| BIBLE | EVENT | WORLD | EVENT |

????—Creation of the world; Adam and Eve. Date unknown. Many conservative Christians date the creation of the world between 5000 BC and 4000 BC.

???

????—Cain and Abel

????—Noah and the Flood (early date)

????—Tower of Babel (early date)

????—Invention of the wheel
????—Invention of pottery

????—Development of sailing ships

3200

????—Development of the Sumerian alphabet (if Flood is at early date)

????—Early Egyptian dynasties founded (if Flood is at early date)

2700

2300—Noah and the Flood (late date)

????—Tower of Babel (late date)

2200

2300—Archaeological evidence points to the practice of cannibalism
2215—The death of Sargon

????—Silk creation begins in China
2200—First editions of the *Epic of Gilgamesh*
2200—Egyptians begin worshipping Ra, the sun god

2166—Birth of Abraham

????—Life of Job

All dates are uncertain.

CHAPTER 2

THE WORLD TAKES SHAPE

THE AGE OF THE PATRIARCHS
2200–1500 BC

As we progress in our study of ancient history, it is essential to recognize that we cannot truly understand the world around us without understanding the Bible as well. The Bible does not merely give us a record of religious and historical events; it actually provides us with a view of the world that we need to comprehend everything around us in the present age. Without understanding what God created and what happened to this creation, we will never truly understand why the events of the world have played out as they have. The world has been shaped by some very pivotal events, and these events are recorded in scripture. When we read the Bible, we are introduced to these turning points, as well as to God's plan for redeeming creation for His glory.

We have already learned about several of these world-changing events, but two—the fall of mankind and the Tower of Babel—are especially important, and we would benefit from a second look before moving on to other events in history.

THE FALL OF MANKIND

When God created the world, He created it good. This means it was free of problems, it contained everything necessary, and it lacked nothing. In its nature and structure, it was perfect and it operated perfectly within its design.

Adam and Eve were designated as stewards of the earth. They had one very simple role in this perfect, divinely created world: to obey God. God wanted them to care for and populate the earth, and to stay away from one particular tree. God did not command them to stay away from this tree because the tree was intrinsically bad. This tree, the tree of the knowledge of good and evil, was like the rest of creation—perfect and without error. Instead, the issue at stake was whether Adam and Eve would love God and express that love through obedience.

The reality, as Francis Schaeffer clearly states in his book *Genesis in Space and Time*, was that Adam did not face a choice between good and evil, but a choice of whether or not he would love God and stay within the bounds that God had established. In choosing to eat from the tree, Adam chose to disobey God and to seek a life outside of God. It is in this act of disobedience that

Expulsion from the Garden of Eden, by Thomas Cole (1828)

Adam chose evil. The heart behind this act is the same heart that is passed to every generation.

The consequence of Adam's choice was that he and Eve would be separated from union with God, and thus they became spiritually dead and started the process of physical death. These consequences were also passed from generation to generation.

How does this help us understand the world around us? One of the main internal consequences of being separated from God is that mankind loses any and all purpose in life. Only when people are walking in union with God do they find their meaning and purpose in being alive, because God created us to have purpose.

Thus, at every new birth, a quest begins—a search for meaning. As people grow, they seek meaning from money, pleasure, status, religion, mysticism, self-actualization, and anything else from which they think they might find fulfillment. Meaning and purpose are sought after in a metaphysical sense, a material sense, and a religious sense. Yet outside of the redemption found only in Jesus Christ, there is no true fulfillment or ultimate meaning. As men and women seek meaning outside the bounds that God has established, it isn't that they have lost their desire for spirituality but that they now want to find it outside of God.

Stained glass window from the Chartres Cathedral, France

AS WE LOOK AT THE WORLD, IT BECOMES CLEAR THAT PEOPLE HAVE SOUGHT MEANING AND PURPOSE THROUGH WAR, MATERIALISM, POWER, PRESTIGE, AND DOMINANCE OVER OTHERS; YET NONE OF THESE THINGS ULTIMATELY SATISFIES. THEREFORE, THE QUEST CONTINUES WITHOUT ANY RESOLUTION. MANKIND HAS ALSO CREATED ALL KINDS OF RELIGIONS AND RELIGIOUS EXPERIENCES. IT IS ONLY BY LOOKING AT THE WORLD THROUGH THE LENS OF THE FALL THAT WE CAN UNDERSTAND WHY THESE QUESTS EXIST AND ARE DOOMED TO FAIL—AND WHERE TO LOOK FOR A SOLUTION THAT WILL ACTUALLY WORK.

THE TOWER OF BABEL

As we've seen, at Babel humans sought to unite as one and to create a way to God that was based on their own merits and standards. But this unity was false because it was not based on being reconciled to God but on a common faith in self-reliance. God intervened and broke up the unity of the people by giving them disparate languages. This is a major reason why the nations of the world do not get along and why there never seems to be a strong sense of commonality among them.

If you were to tour all the nations of the world, you would find that cultural barriers exist in the way that people think and process the world around them. Cultural differences are seen in the way that families operate, the way children are raised, how weddings and other ceremonies are performed, how music is played, and so forth. Even though every human has the same fundamental pursuits in life, there is a difference in the way those pursuits are expressed. It is important to remember, however, that these cultural barriers were put in place by God to slow down the rate of rebellion and keep human pride in check.

The only way that these cultural barriers can be overcome is by gaining a new life in Christ.

Wilhelm von Kaulbach's mural in the stairwell of the new museum in Berlin, Verlag Alexander Dunckel, 1871

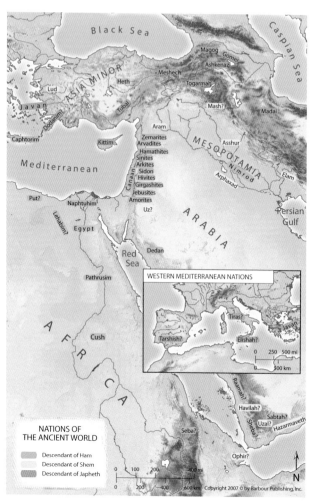

NATIONS OF
THE ANCIENT WORLD

Descendant of Ham
Descendant of Shem
Descendant of Japheth

WESTERN MEDITERRANEAN NATIONS

Copyright 2007 © by Barbour Publishing, Inc.

Only God can truly overcome the barriers that He Himself put in place to divide humanity. It is only through Christ that world peace can be achieved. When believers in Jesus gather, they experience the unity that the world outside of Christ tries to experience but cannot.

All the events that have occurred in history cannot be understood without first comprehending what happened in the Bible. The Bible explains the ultimate purpose of creation and what happened to distort that purpose, as well as the consequences that we experience every day.

With that in mind, let us turn our attention to a very critical moment in world history, the moment when a nation was created that shaped the entire future of the world; that is, the establishment of Israel.

FROM ONE MAN COMES A NATION

The nation of Israel was not formed by simply collecting together a group of people; it came about through the calling of a single man, Abram, and his family (Genesis 12). When we first encounter Abram (later renamed Abraham by God; see Genesis 17:5) in the Bible, the world after the Flood had once again become established, the Fertile Crescent had been repopulated, and the city of Ur had emerged as a prominent center of life. Archaeologists have uncovered evidence that this city and civilization were very sophisticated.

UR: ABRAHAM'S HOMETOWN

Abraham was born in Ur, which was located in ancient Sumer (modern-day southern Iraq). The city's patron deity was Nanna, the Sumerian moon god, and the name of the city is derived from a variant spelling of this god's name. The city today is marked by the ruins of the Great Ziggurat of Ur, which contained the shrine of Nanna and was the center of religious life in the city during Abraham's time. Here, sacrifices were offered to Nanna, and taxes and tithes were collected.

> Archaeologists have uncovered evidence that this city and civilization were very sophisticated.

During Abraham's life, Ur was the center of political power in southeast Mesopotamia. The king of Ur won control of the nearby city of Akkad and

The sacred area in the center of the city of Ur. The ziggurat and the adjacent buildings were dedicated to the moon god Nanna, and they were the economic hub of Ur. Artist: Balage Balogh, 2010.

laid the groundwork for growth and prosperity in the region. During this time, the Ziggurat of Ur was built, and the city became a booming center for commerce and trade. Thus, Abraham lived in a very developed society. This is what makes his move from Ur to Canaan so remarkable. Abraham left Ur during its economic and political pinnacle to move to a land that was rough and undeveloped. We will return to this important event later in the chapter.

Excavations have revealed that the city of Ur was laid out in a rather haphazard manner, yet the houses were not at all what some might expect. Their structure and layout represent rather sophisticated planning. The houses were engineered in a manner that showed attention to space planning, climate control, and functionality. Each house had a courtyard in its interior, and in this courtyard was a drain that collected the rainwater into a cistern for storage. In some of the wealthy homes, evidence has been found of pipes that distributed the collected water throughout the house—one of the earliest examples of indoor plumbing.

While the nation enjoyed such technological advancements, it also faced much political strife. During Abraham's youth, Ur faced potential war with the neighboring cities of

EGYPT IN THE BIBLE

• City established during the Greco-Roman Era

Isin and Larsa. Some scholars speculate that Abraham's father moved the entire family to Haran to escape this looming conflict (Genesis 11).

Yet Ur was not the only place in the world experiencing significant development at the time. The entire world was making major social and technological advances.

For more details on Abraham's move from Ur, read Genesis 10–12.

EGYPT

Although through most of recorded history Egypt has been a unified nation, this was not always the case. Long before Abraham was born, the land we now call Egypt consisted of two separate kingdoms: Lower Egypt and Upper Egypt. Lower Egypt was located at the mouth of the Nile River, where it empties into the Mediterranean Sea. Upper Egypt was located upstream, to the south, in the higher elevations through which the Nile flows from its headwaters in East Africa. Before Abraham was born, Egypt went through a process of unification that formed the basis for its emergence on the world scene during Abraham's time.

The Lower Egyptians were ruled by a king distinguished by his red crown, whereas the Upper Egyptians were ruled by a king named Narmer, who wore a white crown. These two rival kingdoms fought many battles against each other until an epic final battle in which King Narmer attacked the Lower Egyptian king and was victorious. After this decisive victory, Narmer took the red crown of the Lower Egyptian king and placed it over his white crown. With this symbolic gesture, he announced that he was now king over the entire land of Egypt. From this point forward, all kings of Egypt wore the double crown.

Pharaoh depicted with the double crown of Upper and Lower Egypt

> The reason for embalming was that the ancient Egyptians believed the dead could only enter the afterlife if their bodies were preserved.

The unification of Egypt is important because it marks the beginning of a new period in history. There is some debate between Christian and secular historians as to the date that this unification occurred. If we assume a date of approximately 2300 BC for the Flood (see chapter 1), it means that the unification of Egypt must have occurred some time after that. Yet most secular scholars date the unification of Egypt at around 3100 BC. Other conservative scholars, however, suggest that the commonly accepted date for Egypt's unification is erroneously based on ancient lists of kings. They argue that those who made these lists often misrepresented the lengths of reigns of various kings in an attempt to create a more powerful image of certain rulers.

Whatever the exact date for Egypt's unification, it was after this event that the nation recorded its history in hieroglyphics. (These ancient symbols were the first step toward a written alphabet.) It was also during this time that the Egyptians began to formulate their concept of the divine kingship of

Egyptian antiquity from the Louvre Museum

the pharaohs; and it was the era in which the great pyramids were built, along with many other structures that have fascinated mankind for centuries.

After the unification of the nation, Egypt became very rich and powerful. This era is often called the Old Kingdom of Egypt, and it was the period in which the Egyptians began to embalm their dead kings and turn them into mummies. Mummies were the bodies of the deceased, treated with spices and salts and wrapped in linen to keep them from decaying. The reason for embalming was that the ancient Egyptians believed the dead could only enter the afterlife if their bodies were preserved.

The process of embalming was very complicated, and only priests were able to perform this task. After a king died, his body was taken by the priests to the holy place of the temple to be embalmed. There the body would be washed with wine and spices. Then the priests would take all the organs out of the body— including the liver, stomach, lungs, and intestines—and cover them with spices to preserve them. The chief priest also removed the heart, washed it, wrapped it in linen strips, and placed it back inside the dead king's chest.

The Egyptians believed that when the king reached the afterlife, the god Osiris would weigh his heart on a special scale. If his heart was good, it would be light, and the king would spend the rest of the afterlife in happiness. But if his heart was full of sin, it would be heavy and would be devoured by the demon Ammut.

After the priests were finished with the heart, they covered the king's body with salt and more spices, and then waited for forty days. During this period, the people mourned the death of their king. After the forty days had passed, the priests again uncovered the body and organs, and washed them again with oil

The Embalming Process

The body is cleaned and purified.

Natron (a natural salt) is used to dry the body—both inside and out.

The body's internal organs are removed and placed in canopic jars.

The body is wrapped while a priest reads enchantments, which are believed to protect the individual from evil spirits during the journey into the afterlife.

Anubis, supervisor of the mummification process. Underneath the lion bed are the four canopic vases for the organs that were mummified separately. From a wooden sarcophagus, Egypt, ca. 400 BC.

and spices. At this point, the liver, stomach, lungs, and intestines were placed into four jars called canopic jars. Each jar had the image of a god on its lid. The Egyptians believed that these gods would protect the king's organs.

The priests then wrapped the king's body in strips of linen, with special pieces of jewelry placed between the strips. The jewelry was supposed to offer protection for the king as he passed into the afterlife. The priests made a mask of gold that bore a perfect resemblance to the king and put it on his mummy's face, so that the gods would recognize the mummified king when he arrived. After this, a ritual was performed that was believed to allow the king to hear, see, and talk in the afterlife.

Finally, the mummy of the king was placed into three nested coffins. The first was a coffin of gold with the face of the king on the outside. The gold coffin was then placed into a wood coffin to protect it. Finally the wood coffin was placed into a sarcophagus located in a pyramid. Before the priests left the pyramid, they put furniture, jewelry, clothes, toys, games, scrolls, and food in the burial chamber so that the king would have things to do and items to make him feel comfortable in the afterlife.

As we consider the elaborate burial process described above, it becomes evident that mankind has always been concerned with such things as life after death, atonement for sin, and judgment and consequences for sins that remain unredeemed. Man's spiritual quest is intense and pervasive. The intricate process of mummification is an expression of mankind's quest to understand and respond to the divine world.

The pyramids were important structures that were central to the belief system of the ancient Egyptians. The Egyptian kings, called pharaohs, believed that they were divine and thus held a special place of leadership in the world. The pyramids were created as their final resting places. The pyramid's unique shape was believed to assist the pharaohs in their transference from this life to the afterlife.

Above: Anubis conducts the weighing on the scale of Maat against the feather of truth. The ibis-headed Thoth, scribe of the gods, records the result. If his heart is lighter than the feather, Hunefer is allowed to pass into the afterlife. If not, it is eaten by the waiting chimeric creature Ammut, which is composed of the deadly crocodile, lion, and hippopotamus. In the next panel, showing the scene after the weighing, a triumphant Hunefer, having passed the test, is presented by falcon-headed Horus to the shrine of the green-skinned Osiris, god of the underworld and the dead, accompanied by Isis and Nephthys. The fourteen gods of Egypt are shown seated above, in the order of judges.
Below: Pyramids of Giza, Egypt

AS WE CONSIDER THE BELIEF SYSTEM OF ANCIENT EGYPT, WE CAN SEE WHY THERE WAS SUCH A POWER STRUGGLE BETWEEN GOD AND PHARAOH DURING THE TIME OF MOSES. IF PHARAOH BELIEVED HE WAS A DIVINE RULER, THEN WHY WOULD HE SUBMIT TO THE GOD OF MOSES? ONE CAN EASILY UNDERSTAND HOW HIS EGO WOULD BE CHALLENGED BY A CALL TO OBEY YAHWEH, THE GOD OF ISRAEL.

Above: King Tut's burial mask. Right: Stained glass window of Abraham. Original location of window is unknown.

At this point, let's return to an observation that was alluded to earlier. Genesis 1:26 states that God created man in His image. Therefore, mankind has a stamp of the divine on him. Man is not divine in nature but bears a resemblance to the divine. Even though Adam and Eve rebelled against God and brought sin into the world, mankind still has a sense of the divine image. The sin of Adam and Eve, at its core, was a sin of submission—they did not want to live within the boundaries that God had established. Their rebellion does not mark the end of this quest; rather, it marks the beginning of mankind's search for the divine outside of the one true God.

WHEN WE LOOK AT ANCIENT EGYPT, WE SEE AN ILLUSTRATION OF MAN'S PURSUIT OF THE UPWARD CALL OF HIS DIVINE STAMP OUTSIDE OF RELATIONSHIP WITH THE ONE TRUE GOD, YAHWEH. WE ALSO SEE THE EGYPTIANS SEEKING TO ANSWER THE MOST PROFOUND SPIRITUAL QUESTIONS OF LIFE:

- DOES GOD EXIST?
- WHAT HAPPENS WHEN WE DIE?
- HOW DO WE ATONE FOR OUR SIN?
- WILL THERE BE A JUDGMENT?
- CAN THE ETERNAL DWELL WITHIN THE TEMPORAL?
- ARE THERE REWARDS FOR ACTS DONE IN THIS LIFE?

CANAAN

In Genesis 12:1–3, Abraham is called by God to leave his home and go to a land that God would one day give to his descendants. It is important to note that Abraham was not called to start a new religion; he was being called to start a nation. Thus, Abraham's move to a new land was part of the process of providing a homeland for this new people.

For Abraham to move away from Ur at this time would have seemed very illogical. As already noted, the land of Canaan, where Abraham was going, was not as developed as Ur or Haran. Therefore, Abraham must have looked like a fool when he told people that he was leaving the sophisticated world of Mesopotamia for the seemingly backward country of Canaan, which had the reputation of being a barbaric region where people ate raw meat and did not bury their dead. There is no real proof that these ancient stereotypes were true, but it was nevertheless the reputation assigned to Canaan. In fact, as archaeologists have excavated Canaan, they have found that it was marked by very advanced agricultural development.

The land called Canaan was inhabited by the descendants of Noah's grandson Canaan. Genesis 10:15–19 lists the names of many tribes descended from Canaan, including the Hittites, Jebusites, Amorites, Girgashites, and Hivites. The Amorites were among the earliest inhabitants of the land of Canaan. They were an ancient Semitic people that had roots in Canaan, migrated to Mesopotamia, and eventually came back to settle in Canaan.

Canaan has a wide range of landscapes, from the lush hills of Meron in Upper Galilee
in northern Israel (left) to the dry, desert areas of southern Judah (right).

Developments in Canaan

In terms of political power, Canaan comprised many individual city-states rather than a larger, regional power. The industry of each city primarily served itself. Thus, Canaan remained somewhat politically separate from the more global communities of Mesopotamia and Egypt.

Abraham's migration to Canaan took place during the time period called the Bronze Age by historians. It is called the Bronze Age because it was during this time that bronze began to be used as the metal of choice for everything from pots and pans to weaponry. As the Bronze Age developed in Canaan, we can see the progressive urbanization of its city-states.

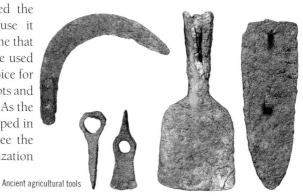

Ancient agricultural tools

Canaan was very fertile during this time, and the weather was perfect for farming. Its inhabitants grew grain, grapes, figs, olives, legumes, onions, cucumbers, and a host of other crops.

Contrary to stereotypes of the time, the Canaanites were a sophisticated agricultural and urban people. They had inhabited the land for at least five hundred years before the Israelites arrived, and they had absorbed and assimilated the features of many different cultures of the ancient Near East.

> Contrary to stereotypes of the time, the Canaanites were a sophisticated agricultural and urban people.

One of the more unique advancements that came from Canaan was the solidification of the alphabet originally developed in Egypt. In Canaan, the alphabet shifted from a picture-based code to a symbol-based code. Instead of a picture that illustrated an object or an idea, each letter became a symbol that reflected a sound. This development took place shortly after the time of Abraham.

Phoenicia (in what is now Lebanon) was an ancient civilization located north of Canaan. It was settled during the time of Abraham and grew into a maritime trading culture. It did not take long for its influence to spread across the Mediterranean during the period from 1550 to 300 BC. Given the great influence of this region, the development of the alphabet in Phoenicia around 1050 BC had an impact on the entire world, and its influence is still felt today in virtually every alphabet of Western civilization, including Greek, Hebrew, Aramaic, Latin, and Arabic. Even the modern English alphabet traces its roots to the Phoenician alphabet.

𐤀	'	𐤕	T	𐤐	P
𐤁	B	𐤉	Y	𐤒	C
𐤂	G	𐤊	K	𐤒	Q
𐤃	D	𐤋	L	𐤓	R
𐤄	H	𐤌	M	𐤔	Ś, Š
𐤅	W	𐤍	N	𐤕	Th
𐤆	Z	𐤎	S		
𐤇	Ch	𐤏	'		

The Phoenician alphabet

A clay figurine, possibly of the goddess Asherah

The Canaanites practiced what has been called an agricultural religion. At the heart of this religion were fertility rituals. Their main gods were called the Baalim (lords), and their wives the Baalot (ladies) or Ashtoret (sometimes known by the singular form Asherah). The Canaanites believed that if they pleased their gods, the gods would send the rain that the people needed for survival; if they displeased the gods, their crops would fail. They believed that by following certain rituals, they would be in harmony with the world and the gods of this world. The rituals they practiced involved immoral sexual practices, the use of sacred temple prostitutes, and a variety of offerings and sacrifices.

This was the world of Canaan—the world that Israel would struggle with for years to come. But things were also happening in parts of the world outside of Mesopotamia, Egypt, and Canaan.

International Trade

One very interesting area of study in this time period is the progress made in international commerce. Commerce is the act of selling and buying goods and commodities. It has always been an obvious reality that the more people there are to buy an individual product, the more potential there is to make a profit. This is one reason why selling goods outside of one's own community has been a constant pursuit throughout world history. As the world became increasingly more populated, trade grew in scale to become a greater force in people's lives.

BY FAR THE EASIEST METHOD FOR TRANSPORTING GOODS WAS BY WATER. THIS WAS ESPECIALLY TRUE IN AN ERA WHEN TOWNS AND VILLAGES WERE LINKED BY FOOTPATHS RATHER THAN WELL-MAINTAINED ROADS. THE FIRST EXTENSIVE TRADE ROUTES DEVELOPED UP AND DOWN THE GREAT RIVERS. THESE RIVERS BECAME THE BACKBONE OF EARLY CIVILIZATIONS—THE NILE RIVER, THE TIGRIS AND EUPHRATES RIVERS, THE INDUS RIVER, AND THE HWANG HO (YELLOW RIVER). FROM THE EARLIEST TIMES, TRADE CENTERED ON THE CITIES THAT WERE SCATTERED ALONG THE GREAT RIVERS OF THE WORLD.

As boats became sturdier, coastal trade extended between more distant areas. The eastern Mediterranean was the first region to develop extensive maritime trade, first between Egypt and Minoan Crete, and later in the ships of the intrepid Phoenicians.

The Phoenicians were famous not only for the spread of the alphabet among the nations of the world but also for their luxury goods. Phoenician cedar was exported as top-quality timber for architecture and shipbuilding. Phoenicia's rare and expensive purple dye was highly sought after throughout the known world. The region also became famous for its metalwork, particularly in gold, and the Phoenician cities of Tyre and Sidon were known for their glass.

THE BRONZE AGE

The Bronze Age brought about some interesting advancements in military equipment. Of special note is the development of the chariot. The first chariots appeared in Mesopotamia shortly before the birth of Abraham. The original chariot was a fast, light vehicle that consisted of an open two- or four-wheeled car. The car was basically a semicircular framework with a waist-high guard covering the front and sides. Chariots were used primarily for warfare during the Bronze and Iron Ages, though they could be used for travel as well. As warfare evolved, chariots began to be replaced by cavalry and were relegated primarily to entertainment purposes (for example, the chariot races depicted in *Ben-Hur*).

Above: An artist's rendition of a Greek phalanx. Though the armor and weaponry would have been slightly different in the Bronze Age, the basic concept and formation are the same. Below: Bronze Age chariot drawn from remains found in Nineveh. From *Nineveh and Its Palaces* by Joseph Bonomi (1853).

There is much debate as to the exact role that chariots played in warfare, because we have little historical record about their early use. Most historians believe that chariots were used as mobile firing platforms for archers. Evidence suggests that during the early Bronze Age, battles were fought mainly by infantry. Spearmen were equipped with long spears and arranged in a formation of soldiers marching into battle in the shape of a large box. Later, the Greeks would adapt this technique and call it a *phalanx*.

Another major achievement from this era was the domestication of cats. By the time Abraham's grandson Jacob was living in Canaan, the Egyptians had trained cats to catch snakes.

After Joseph, the son of Jacob, was sold into slavery in Egypt, he eventually rose to a position of leadership there, and he relocated his entire extended family to Egypt. This move was partially brought about by the family's efforts to escape a severe famine that ravaged the Near East, including Canaan. Egypt, under the leadership of Joseph, was prepared for the famine and was thus an ideal place for Joseph's family.

For more details on Joseph in Egypt, read Genesis 39–50.

After Joseph died, there was a leadership change in Egypt. The new king did not like the potential threat that the growing Israelite population posed in Egypt, so he began to enslave them. This dark era of servitude for the Israelites stood in marked contrast to a period of literary advancement that was being experienced by the Egyptians during this time.

Ancient Egyptian literature had grown out of their religious beliefs, but over time it also came to address topics related to man's ordinary, day-to-day life. Literature held a distinguished position in ancient Egyptian thought and

Israel in Egypt, painted by Edward Poynter in 1867. Oil on canvas.

civilization. The ancient Egyptians viewed literature as a source of spiritual nourishment as well as entertainment. Writing as an art was well developed in Egyptian culture. The scope of Egyptian writing during this time was extensive and included such genres as novels, short stories, poetry, folklore, proverbs, wise sayings, moral teachings, philosophical meditations, and literary messages.

> The ancient Egyptians viewed literature as a source of spiritual nourishment as well as entertainment.

HAMMURABI OF BABYLON

During the time when the Israelites lived as slaves in Egypt, the world was continuing to change and develop. Power struggles continued in Mesopotamia; unlike Egypt, the region was unstable and in a constant state of war. Powerful leaders sought to expand their empires through warfare and enslavement. Over time, cities were conquered and various empires rose and fell.

Around 1792 BC, a king named Hammurabi inherited the throne of Babylon from his father. At first, Hammurabi ruled over a small area of land immediately surrounding his city. Over time, however, he began to conquer other small cities in the region. Hammurabi leveraged his growing power to convince other cities to swear allegiance to him in order to avoid blood-shed. Soon Hammurabi ruled over the entire southern part of Mesopotamia. It was during his reign that this region received the name Babylonia.

Hammurabi was a unique ruler in that he did not use his military strength as the force to convince people to follow him. After gaining control over a region, Hammurabi sought to establish a rule of law that would govern his empire. He taught the people that the chief god of Babylon, Murduk, had established his throne and had given him the power to rule for the purpose of treating people fairly. Hammurabi placed a high priority on the establishment of justice in the land. Thus, he established a set of laws that he believed were just, and all citizens were required to obey them. Hammurabi's code of 282 laws brought order to his empire and allowed him to rule in a more efficient manner.

Hammurabi marble bas-relief, one of twenty-three reliefs of great historical lawgivers in the chamber of the House of Representatives in the United States Capitol. Sculpted by Thomas Hudson Jones in 1950.

The Code of Hammurabi is considered one of the earliest sets of written civil codes that has ever been found. The scope of these codes applied to everyone in the land, whether rich, poor, free, or

Code of Hammurabi

enslaved. They covered a wide range of topics, including family life and civic responsibility. Here are some of the codes:

Code of Hammurabi on display at the Louvre Museum

- If a man kills another man's son, his son shall be cut off.

- If anyone ensnares another for a crime which he cannot prove, then he that ensnared him shall be put to death.

- If someone cuts down a tree on someone else's land, he shall pay for it.

- If anyone brings an accusation of any crime before the elders and does not prove what he has charged, he shall, if a capital offense is charged, be put to death.

- If a builder builds a house for someone and does not construct it properly, and the house which he built falls in and kills its owner, then the builder shall be put to death. (Another variant of this code is that if the owner's son dies, then the builder's son shall be put to death.)

- If a son slaps his father, his hand shall be cut off.

- If a robber is caught breaking a hole into a house so that he can get in and steal, he will be put to death in front of the hole.

- If anyone steals the young son of another, he shall be put to death.

- If someone is careless when watering his fields and he floods someone else's field by accident, he will pay for the grain he has ruined.

- If a man strikes a pregnant woman, thereby causing her to miscarry and die, the assailant's daughter shall be put to death.

- If a man puts out the eye of another man, his eye shall be put out.

AT THE CORE OF ALL OF HAMMURABI'S CODES IS THE EXECUTION OF JUSTICE. HAMMURABI BELIEVED THAT THE BEST WAY TO RULE A NATION WAS TO ESTABLISH LAWS THAT PRESERVED AND PROTECTED JUSTICE. IN THE PREAMBLE TO HIS CODES, HE STATED THAT ONE OF THE GOALS OF HIS LAW WAS TO MAKE SURE THAT THE STRONG DID NOT OVER-POWER THE WEAK.

> At the center of every human heart, in every part of the world, a value is placed on justice. Justice is not simply a Western notion. . . . All cultures value some form of justice.

One of the ways that justice was enforced was by following a principle that was later called *lex talionis* (Latin for "the law of retribution"). According to this principle, if a person committed a certain crime, a similar action could be taken against him or her. Once that like action was taken, there was no allowance for reciprocation. Therefore, if a man killed the child of another man, the child of the murderer would be killed. However, the murderer would not be allowed to reciprocate this act and kill anyone else. The ultimate goals of the principle of lex talionis were to carry out justice for wrongdoing and to deter future wrongdoing, since potential offenders would know that they would be subject to the same harm.

What would make a king so desirous to ensure that justice ruled? Here is where the Bible helps us understand the world. The Bible states that every human being is created in the image of God (Genesis 1:26–27), and as such we bear the mark of our Creator. One of the core moral traits of our Creator is justice. This shows us why the early moral codes found in the nations of the world had at their core a serving of some type of justice.

At the center of every human heart, in every part of the world, a value is placed on justice. Justice is not simply a Western notion. Interpretations and expressions of justice vary depending on the cultural setting (keep in mind that at the Tower of Babel, God created different cultures), yet all cultures value some form of justice. Go to any culture and steal another man's wife, and you will see how the husband will want justice regardless of where he lives or in what culture.

In addition to establishing a rule of law over the land, Hammurabi also dug a great canal between Kish and the Persian Gulf, which irrigated a large area of land and protected the southern cities from the flooding of the Tigris.

Hammurabi sought to solidify his leadership by connecting it with the will of the gods. He constructed temples and established a clergy base, and he supported them through taxation. Out of his taxes, he not only fortified his government and army but also enforced his codes.

REFLECTIONS

During the time of Abraham and his descendants, the world continued to experience major developments that have shaped all societies ever since. Egypt became a superpower, Canaan developed agriculturally, and Hammurabi established a society run by laws based on the serving of justice. At the same time, we can see God's imprint on the world. We see mankind seeking justice and order. We see humans using the skills God gave them to subdue the world. But we also see the wars, conflicts, and misery that sin brought into the world. Even as God divided the world into its regions, and people expressed themselves in different

cultural manners, we still see man's quest for meaning and purpose, his attempt to deal with sin, and his desire to establish justice. The world had truly taken shape.

TIME LINE
2200 BC – 1500 BC

BIBLE EVENT   WORLD EVENT

2200

2166—Birth of Abraham

2100—Ziggurat built in Ur

2080—Birth of Ishmael
2066—Birth of Isaac
2005—Birth of Jacob

2000

1950—Amorites conquer Mesopotamia
1940—City of Ur falls

1914—Birth of Joseph
1884—Joseph's rise in Egypt
1876—Joseph's family moves to Egypt

1800

1766—Shang dynasty begins in China
1750—Code of Hammurabi created

?????—Israelites enslaved in Egypt

1600

1600—Hittites defeat Babylon; rise of Hittites

1526—Birth of Moses

All dates are approximate.

CHAPTER 3

THE ESTABLISHMENT OF ISRAEL

AN IMPORTANT DISCOVERY
1500–1000 BC

It was just an average day for an average peasant woman in Tell el-Amarna, Egypt. The year was 1887, and this day began as most. Yet sometimes an average person on an average day can intersect with an extraordinary moment in history and be part of something that will open the world's eyes to a new understanding of itself. On this warm Egyptian day, that is exactly what happened.

This woman, about whom we know virtually nothing—not even her name—was doing something she had done countless times before in her life. She was digging for residue from the bricks of ancient ruins to get fertilizer for her crops. The mud that was used to form the bricks of ancient buildings contained bits of fertilizer, so farmers during the nineteenth century often fertilized their crops by finding bricks from ancient ruins, crushing them into a fine dust, and sprinkling the dust on their crops.

On this typical day, this ordinary peasant woman made an extraordinary

North Palace at Tell el-Amarna

discovery. She found tablets from a portion of the royal archives of ancient Egypt. When she first dug up the tablets, she was unaware of what she had found. She filled her basket with the tablets and went home. No one knows how many she pulled from the site or how many she had already crushed and sprinkled on her garden, but at some point she realized she had unearthed something very special. She set the remaining tablets aside, knowing that a find like this was worth some money.

In Egypt during this time, archaeologists from both England and France were digging around the country looking for ancient cities and ruins in order to learn about earlier generations. When the peasant woman first attempted to sell her tablets to some European scholars, she was accused of forgery (a common practice due to the high demand at that time for ancient relics) and sent away. Apparently, it seemed unthinkable to the scholars that anything of this importance would be found in such a casual manner.

At this point, the tablets were taken to Luxor and sold to tourists. It is unclear whether the woman sold them herself or sold them to a dealer. Many of the tablets were destroyed as she made her way to Luxor. Finally, the British Museum learned of the tablets, realized their priceless value, and purchased most of them. News of the amazing find led archaeologists to identify and excavate the entire region in which the tablets were found, and between 1891 and 1892 more tablets were discovered. These tablets are now known as the Amarna Letters, drawing their name from the place of their original discovery in Tell el-Amarna, Egypt.

WHAT IS SO EXCITING ABOUT THESE TABLETS, AND WHY ARE THEY OF INTEREST TO US TODAY? THESE TABLETS WERE ANCIENT LETTERS WRITTEN TO EGYPT FROM VARIOUS CITY-STATES IN CANAAN, AND THEY ADDRESS A MULTIPLICITY OF ISSUES. SOME WERE WRITTEN IN BABYLONIAN CUNEIFORM DURING THE TIME OF MOSES AND JOSHUA. THEY ALSO PROVIDE THE FIRST EXTRABIBLICAL EVIDENCE OF THE HEBREW TRIBES ENTERING THE LAND OF CANAAN. SOME OF THE TABLETS WERE ANXIOUS LETTERS WRITTEN FROM JERUSALEM (URUSALIM), WARNING THE PHARAOH OF AN INVASION BY THE HABIRU (KHABIRU), WHO WERE APPROACHING FROM THE TRANSJORDAN.

One of the Amarna Letters, in this case a cuneiform tablet from Tushratta, king of Mitanni, to the pharaoh Amenhotep III, ca. 1350 BC. This letter contains a negotiation of marriage between the pharaoh and Tushratta's daughter Tadukhipa.

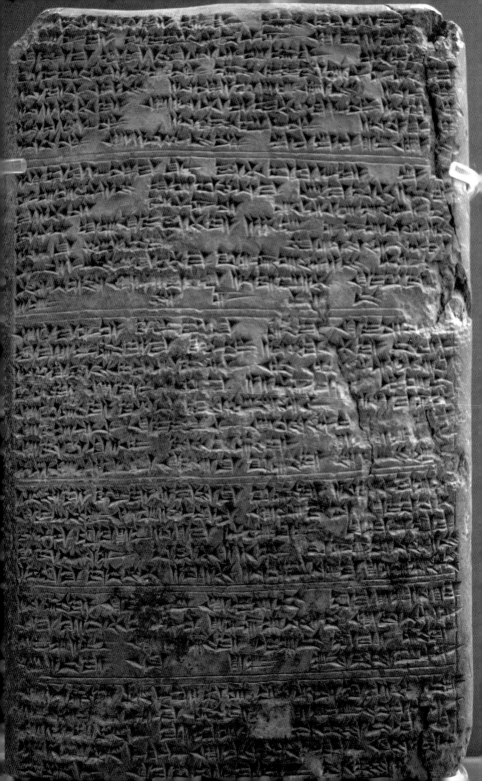

> These letters give us insight into the great international distress the Hebrews caused by taking over the promised land.

These letters give us insight into the great international distress the Hebrews caused by taking over the promised land. The hand of God was with the Israelites, and God made His power known throughout the world as He blessed the efforts of His people. Therefore, the surrounding nations were afraid of what God was doing.

THE CONQUEST OF CANAAN

When we talk about fearing God, it is important to recognize that this can refer to two different things. One kind of fear recognizes how great God is and seeks to show Him the honor and the reverence that are due His name.

Ruins of ancient Jericho

Another quakes in the presence of God's great power, but it does not lead to giving Him praise and honor. The Amarna Letters show us that the inhabitants of Canaan were indeed afraid of the power that surrounded the Israelites, but their fear was of the second type, since it does not appear to have led to worship of the Lord.

For more on Israel's conquest, read Numbers and Joshua.

Out of this fear, many within Canaan began to write to Egypt for help, requesting immediate military assistance in dealing with these fierce invaders. One letter from the city of Megiddo mentions that several towns located in the region of Arad in the south had already fallen to the invaders. According to Numbers 21:1–3, the Israelites destroyed many cities in this southern region before they moved north along the eastern side of the Dead Sea, crossed the Jordan River, and entered Canaan to begin their conquest.

One fascinating point regarding these letters is that none were found from the first cities destroyed during the Israelite invasion (Jericho and Ai). This supports the notion that Israel began its invasion by destroying these two cities, which caused the rest of the cities to become afraid.

Prior to Israel's entrance into Canaan, the region seems to have been organized around major cities that established small principalities. These cities were independent of each other and were not organized centrally for defense. This helped the Israelites as they entered the land, because the Canaanites could not fight them with a unified national army. Instead, the Israelites had only to conquer individual, autonomous cities. Once a city fell, the Israelites could simply move on to take the next city.

THE GOD EL

Life in Canaan was similar to life in many other places in the surrounding region. Archaeology has revealed that religion was very important, and much of everyday life was centered on worship practices. Among the more significant archaeological finds were the cuneiform tablets discovered in the royal library and temple in Ugarit. These tablets date from approximately 1400 BC, not long before the final fall of Ugarit in about 1200 BC, and they provide great insight into what life was like in Canaan prior to the Israelite conquest.

Ivory carving of a Canaanite deity, possibly the god El

From the tablets at Ugarit and elsewhere, we learn that El was acknowledged as the head of a pantheon of gods and was regarded as both the creator god and a fertility god.

El was joined by Athirat, apparently his wife, who is represented in the Old Testament as Asherah. Athirat was acknowledged as the mother of the deities, having given birth to some seventy gods and goddesses. Thus, she was predominately a fertility goddess and designated "creatress of the gods."

Even though El was held in high esteem, there were still other gods that played a part in the local worship of Canaan. The people believed that the productivity of their land was predicated on their ability to keep these local deities happy. In Canaanite religion, each city had its own individual master (or *Baal*, which means "master"). These Baals held authority in their respective cities and were the offspring of El. The temple for El was located in the northern region, and it was not possible for everyone to worship at his temple. However, the individual Baals were easily accessible because they were localized gods that came from El. Therefore, fidelity to the Baal was a way to ensure fidelity to El, and this, in turn, would ensure the fertility of the land.

Ancient temple, possibly for Baal

The people in Canaan were very devoted to their gods. It is likely that this was because Canaan was a wonderfully rich land, and the people greatly prospered from it. The Canaanites directly attributed this prosperity to their gods, so it was imperative that they remained loyal to them. In Deuteronomy 6, Yahweh warned the Israelites not to forget Him when they entered the land. He knew that this land was so wonderful and so beautiful that once they entered it, they would be tempted to forget the God who had given it to them.

Depiction of the god Baal. Original artist and date unknown.

■ *"And when the* Lord *your God brings you into the land that he swore to your fathers, to Abraham, to Isaac, and to Jacob, to give you—with great and good cities that you did not build, and houses full of all good things that you did not fill, and cisterns that you did not dig, and vineyards and olive trees that you did not plant—and when you eat and are full, then take care lest you forget the* Lord, *who brought you out of the land of Egypt, out of the house of slavery. It is the* Lord *your God you shall fear. Him you shall serve and by his name you shall swear. You shall not go after other gods, the gods of the peoples who are around you—for the* Lord *your God in your midst is a jealous God—lest the anger of the* Lord *your God be kindled against you, and he destroy you from off the face of the earth"* (Deuteronomy 6:10–15).

It is easy to get caught up in the pleasures of the flesh and to live a life centered on ourselves. Yahweh did not want this for His people and warned them not to fall prey to the pleasures of the land that He was giving them. If they did succumb, they might partake of the religious practices of the

An illustration from the fall of Jericho from a Bible card published in 1901 by the Providence Lithograph Company.

Canaanites and forget the One who had led them from Egypt to the promised land. Sadly, however, the Israelites were drawn away to worship the local gods, and they suffered many consequences for their actions.

ONE STEP FORWARD, TWO STEPS BACK

Yahweh enabled the Israelites to enter the land (see the book of Joshua for details of the conquest), but that does not mean that all went well. The Israelites failed to purge the nation of the Canaanite religion, and thus they began to cohabitate with the people and adopt their religion. Judges 2 records a very discouraging scenario:

■ *And the people of Israel did what was evil in the sight of the* Lord *and served the Baals. And they abandoned the* Lord, *the God of their fathers, who had brought them out of the land of Egypt. They went after other gods, from among the gods of the peoples who were around them, and bowed down to them. And they provoked the* Lord *to anger (Judges 2:11–12).*

The people of Israel did not want to serve God. Instead, they were pulled into the ritual practices of Canaan. This led them to fall into the same type of political and religious structure as the Canaanites. Each city within the land became autonomous, and the people eventually became loyal to the Baals in addition to Yahweh. However, joining the pagan rituals of Canaanite worship to the purity and exclusivity that belong to Yahweh was a great offense to Him.

PART OF WHAT MADE CANAANITE RELIGION SO ABHORRENT TO GOD WAS THE WAY IN WHICH THE CANAANITES WORSHIPPED THEIR GODS. THEIR METHOD OF WORSHIP WAS TIED TO THEIR UNDERSTANDING OF THEIR GODS AS ONES WHO ENSURED THE FERTILITY OF THE LAND AND THE PEOPLE. THIS LED THE PEOPLE TO ENGAGE IN DETESTABLE ACTS, SUCH AS TEMPLE PROSTITUTION, BY WHICH THE WORSHIPPER BELIEVED THAT HE OR SHE WAS UNITING IN THE PROCREATIVE PROCESS AND THUS ACTING SIMILAR TO THE GOD EL OR THE GODDESS ATHIRAT. THIS PERVERTED CUSTOM WAS EVEN PRACTICED BY MANY ISRAELITES, AND IT BROUGHT UPON THEM ALL KINDS OF TROUBLE (SEE THE BOOK OF JUDGES).

It took many centuries for these practices to be re-moved from the land. In fact, the land became so perverted with such worship that, by the time of King Josiah (around 621 BC), even the Temple Mount in Jerusalem contained vessels made for Baal and Asherah. Fortunately, Josiah removed these vessels, as well as the houses of male cult prostitutes (2 Kings 23:1–20).

For more details on King Josiah, read 2 Kings 23.

King Josiah in a seventeenth-century painting by an unknown artist in the choir of Sankta Maria kyrka in Åhus, Sweden

When the Israelites took over Canaan, the balance of power in the world shifted away from Egypt to new countries in the northeast.

Yet even though Israel rebelled against God, this did not stop God from using His people as a light of truth to the world. God will not allow the depravity of the world to stop His plan. He is so powerful that He can carry out His will and bring glory to Himself even through those who sin and rebel against Him (Genesis 50:20; Romans 8:28–29).

This is clearly seen in the nation of Israel. Even though the Canaanites had a strong influence on them, and even though many Israelites rebelled against God, God still used this nation to bring about a Messiah and to bring blessing to the entire world (Matthew 1).

The taking of Canaan by the Israelites marked a very important shift in world power. It was a movement much like the fall of Communism in the late 1980s, when the Soviet Union lost its dominant position of power in the world. In the same way, when the Israelites took over Canaan, the balance of power in the world shifted away from Egypt to new countries in the northeast.

OUT WITH THE OLD, IN WITH THE NEW

One of the realities of life is that, every so often, the balance of power in the world shifts. God never allows one kingdom to get what it ultimately desires—control over the whole world (Psalm 2). Over time, power shifts from one country in one region to another country in another region. The Israelites entered the promised land just as Egypt began its decline as a superpower and Assyria became the dominant power in the ancient Near East.

After the exodus of the Israelites, Egypt went through a period of transformation. A new pharaoh, Amenhotep IV, came to power (ca. 1372–1354 BC), and he subsequently changed his name to Ikhnaton to honor the god Aton.

Ikhnaton transformed Egypt by introducing a major theological change. He abandoned the polytheism that had been embedded in Egyptian culture and embraced monotheism. At the time, monotheism was not a popular form of religion throughout the world, so his religious ideas were somewhat unique.

Engraving that depicts the family of Ikhnaton making an offering to the sun god named Aton

Ikhnaton's fundamental premise was that the sun, named Aton, was the only true god, and that he was Aton's spiritual son. In his theology, he taught that everything had its being through the rays of the sun. In his now famous words, Ikhnaton praised his god as the only great god of the world:

> How numerous are Thy works. They are concealed from the vision of men, O sole of God, other than whom there is no other. Thou hast created the earth according to Thy heart, with men and flocks and all the animals. . . . Thou dost apportion to each man his place, Thou providest for his needs: each has his nourishment, and the hour of his death is fixed. (Ninian Smart, *The Religious Experience of Mankind* [New York: Scribner, 1969], 224)

But Ikhnaton's extreme passion for his religious beliefs was his undoing. He defaced every monument carved with the name of Amon, previously considered the greatest of all the gods of Egypt. At the same time, he failed to inspire the entire nation to follow him, so his religious beliefs were tolerated only for the duration of his reign. The people were outraged by his destruction of their traditions and by his extreme passion for his new beliefs. After his death, his mummy was destroyed, and most references to him were removed from temples and palaces.

Nevertheless, Ikhnaton's reign started a major shift in world power. This power shift is very important as we consider the way in which redemptive history unfolded. At this point in biblical history, the focus shifted from Israel in Egypt to Israel in the promised land. God had delivered Israel from slavery in Egypt and had given His people the land He had promised to them. Now God allowed Ikhnaton's religious zeal to begin the process of weakening the Egyptian Empire.

Ikhnaton neglected the outlying provinces of Egypt, including the province of Canaan. Up to this time, Egypt controlled much of Canaan, though its interest was not so much in occupying the region as it was in ensuring the protection of vital trade routes that passed through the region. As a result of Ikhnaton's inattention, the Israelites

Statue of the god Amon dedicated by King Tutankhamen

began establishing themselves in Canaan with no response from Egypt. In this way, God granted the Israelites protection from Egypt.

In addition to Ikhnaton's religious zeal and political carelessness, it is also reasonable to suggest that the Egyptians would have recognized the power of Yahweh due to the events of the Exodus. God had very clearly shown His power over the Egyptians. Thus, as God's redemptive history shifted its center from Egypt to Canaan, Egypt began a process of decline in world dominance.

A NEW GENERATION OF PHARAOHS

Top: King Tut's golden mask
Bottom: Statues of Rameses II overlooking the Nile. These statues are 67 feet high at Abu Simbel, Egypt.

After Ikhnaton, a new pharaoh by the name of Tutankhamen (or King Tut, as he is affectionately called in the West) reigned over Egypt. Tutankhamen was nine years old when he became pharaoh, and he reigned for approximately ten years. Tutankhamen's significance stems from his rejection of the monotheism of Ikhnaton. He returned Egypt to its original polytheistic beliefs. Another distinction of King Tut's was that his tomb in the Valley of the Kings was discovered almost completely intact—the most complete ancient Egyptian royal tomb ever found.

Tutankhamen was worshipped as a god and honored with a cultlike following during his lifetime. Archaeologists have unearthed ancient Egyptian writings dedicated to Tutankhamen, which indicate that he was appealed to in his deified state for forgiveness and deliverance from problems, sickness, and diseases caused by wrongdoing. Temples of his cult were also built throughout Egypt.

After Tutankhamen, another pharaoh, known as Rameses II, ruled Egypt, and for a time he revived some of the strength and power of the declining nation. Rameses II was a powerful leader who launched extensive rebuilding

Pharaoh Ikhnaton in a pillar of remains of the Aton temple in Karnak. This artifact is now on display at the Egyptian Museum (Cairo, Egypt).

projects and recaptured some of the regions that had been invaded by the Hittites. Yet the cost of his military conquests and rebuilding plans financially strained the nation. Even so, Rameses II reestablished Egypt to the point where it was able to survive and stand strong even as the balance of power began to shift toward Mesopotamia.

Image of Rameses II storming the Hittite fortress of Dapur; from a wall picture on Rameses's temple at Thebes. This reproduction is an illustration from the *Encyclopaedia Biblica* (1903).

Some scholars propose a later date (sometimes called the "Low Date") for the exodus of Israel and suggest that Rameses II was the pharaoh with whom Moses contended. Others place the Exodus earlier (sometimes called the "High Date"). The framework of this book assumes the earlier "High Date."

THE WORLD TAKES A STEP FORWARD

Along with the power shift in the world at this time, another noteworthy advancement was the discovery of iron. After the Israelites entered the land of Canaan and began to settle there during the period of the judges, the Bronze Age came to a close and gave rise to the Iron Age.

Iron Age workers working in a furnace

THE BEGINNING OF THE IRON AGE VARIED GEOGRAPHICALLY AS EACH REGION LEARNED OF IRON'S SUPERIOR STRENGTH AND BEGAN TO REPLACE BRONZE OBJECTS WITH IRON ONES. THE USE OF SMELTED AND TEMPERED IRON BECAME COMMON AMONG THE HITTITES DURING THE PERIOD EXTENDING FROM 1900 TO 1400 BC. IT IS POSSIBLE THAT THE HITTITE KINGS KEPT THEIR IRONWORKING TECHNIQUES SECRET AND RESTRICTED THE EXPORT OF IRON WEAPONS.

After the downfall of the Hittite Empire in 1200 BC, however, the great waves of travelers spreading through southern Europe and the Middle East fueled the rapid spread of iron technology. The oldest-known article of iron shaped by hammering is a dagger found in Egypt that was made before 1350 BC. This dagger is believed to have been of Hittite workmanship.

THE HITTITE EMPIRE

The people of the Iron Age were able to build on the advancements of the Bronze Age and to enjoy the great benefits of iron in their daily lives. Farming became easier as animals were domesticated and new technologies assisted in the cultivation of the land. People were able to make use of forests with greater efficiency as stronger tools for cutting timber were developed. Villages were fortified, and warfare advanced as iron swords and

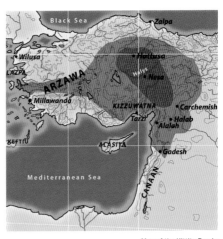

Map of the Hittite Empire

shields began to replace wooden and bronze spears. In short, the world continued to advance as new technologies were discovered and put into common use.

As we consider these advancements in technology and their effect on world cultures, it is important to recognize that God is not only the God of biblical history; He is the God of all history, whether secular, sacred, or redemptive. So why did the world advance as it did during this time? Why did God allow for stonework to give way to bronze and bronze to give way to iron? How do these advancements relate to God and His ultimate purpose for history?

The simple answer is that as much as humanity has rejected God, and as much as God is a God of justice and demands atonement for sin, He is also a God of love and has an eye for the nations. In other words, God truly does love the world and extends grace and mercy to His people in order to give them time to be saved (2 Peter 3:8–10).

God allowed humanity to advance in order to be able to care for itself and live on this planet. As the population grew and new tensions emerged in the world, God gave people the skills and abilities to forge new technologies that were necessary for the people to care for themselves.

Jesus taught this point in His famous body of teaching that we commonly call the Sermon on the Mount (Matthew 5–7):

■ *"You have heard that it was said, 'You shall love your neighbor and hate your enemy.' But I say to you, Love your enemies and pray for those who persecute you, so that you may be sons of your Father who is in heaven. For he makes his sun rise on the evil and on the good, and sends rain on the just and on the unjust. For if you love those who love you, what reward do you have? Do not even the tax collectors do the same? And if you greet only your brothers, what more are you doing than others? Do not even the Gentiles do the same?"* (Matthew 5:43–47).

Jesus said that the Father causes the rain to fall on both the just and the unjust. In other words, God allows both those who are right with Him and those who are in rebellion against Him to live and survive in this world.

The Sermon on the Mount by Carl Heinrich Bloch, nineteenth-century Danish painter

The reason that God does this is that He is loving, caring, and merciful to everyone. This does not mean that everyone in the world will be saved. But God in His mercy will allow people to live in order to allow more opportunity for the message of salvation to be proclaimed to all the earth. Therefore, as we see the world take shape, let us stop and consider the great mercy of God in allowing technology to advance in the world to make life easier and to provide for His people. This is a sign that all people can find mercy at the hand of God.

> **They shared something in common with all religions: the belief that there is more to this life then what we can see.**

OUTSIDE THE NEAR EAST

There was more going on in the world at this time than just in the regions of the Mediterranean Sea and the Near East. In addition to invasions and power shifts in the Middle East, cultural groups from that area were expanding into India.

Among the first groups to invade India were the Aryans, who came out of Iran to the north around 1500 BC. The Aryans brought with them strong cultural traditions that are still a part of Indian culture today. They spoke and wrote in a language called Sanskrit, which was later used in the first documentation of the Vedas, the oldest scriptures of the Hindu religion. The Aryans conquered and defeated the people of the Indus Valley, and subsequently lived among them, introducing the caste system and establishing the foundations of the Indian religion.

There is much speculation about life in India prior to the invasion of the Aryans. Ruins found in the Indus Valley show a very advanced lifestyle. Yet it was not until the Aryan invasion that clear records were kept about the religious practices and life of the people of India.

Though many of the religious ideas that the Aryans introduced to India were new to that part of the world, at their core they still shared something in common with all religions: the belief that there is more to this life than what we can see. In other words, they understood the

The Indus Valley

transcendent nature of life. They also understood that transcendence means there must also be a set of rules that governs this supernatural reality, and this framework is meant to order every aspect of life.

Every religion holds this view in common. Where did such an understanding of the world come from? The Christian scriptures show that it comes from the fact that every human being is created in the image of God and shares in the inner pursuit of the divine. Because of sin, however, humanity will never of its own accord—that is, without being led by Yahweh—pursue Yahweh as God. Instead, humanity will seek the transcendent among other sources. Nevertheless, the human pursuit of the divine provides for a universal understanding of the presence of the supernatural. This same pursuit of the supernatural will take different forms, depending on the culture or group that develops the religion. Yet all pursue the truth in some way.

As we turn our attention from India to other parts of the world, we see that there were also major changes taking place in Greece at this time.  Ancient Greece was entering its Dark Ages (1100–800 BC), which refers to the period of Greek history between the end of the Mycenaean civilization in the eleventh century BC and the rise of the first Greek city-states in the ninth century. The Mycenaean period of Greek history started roughly around 1600 BC and is noted as a civilization dominated by a warrior aristocracy. During

this time, the Greeks took control of Crete and adopted a form of script that became the foundation for the Greek alphabet. It was also during this time that the great city of Troy was defeated.

The collapse of the Mycenaean civilization coincided with the fall of several other large empires in the Near East, most notably the Hittite and Egyptian empires. Many claim that the transition from the Bronze Age to the Iron Age opened the door to a military imbalance. Thus, many nations that were well established, like Greece, were at a disadvantage until they could catch up with those societies that possessed the new advancements in weaponry. Regardless of the reasons for the collapse of various nations, one thing we learn from scripture is that God is ultimately the One who elevates and deposes kings and kingdoms.

A LONG WAY AWAY

Around the time of David (shortly after the period of the Israelite judges), the Mayans of Central America began to expand across the Mesoamerican lowlands. This does not mean that these regions were uninhabited before this time. Rather, it was during this period that the people of this region developed into organized societies and built the temples that many associate with this area.

The Mayans became a very advanced society that developed a sophisticated array of farming implements and cultivated a wide variety of crops, including corn. With the improvements in farming and the invention of greater tools for survival, settlements began to grow, and ceremonial worship centers were built. That these temples were shaped much like the ones found

Ruins of the ancient Mayan city of Palenque

in Ur supports the idea that at some point early in human history, people were scattered from Mesopotamia around the whole world. Also, when you consider that the entire human race springs from one original couple, and that this couple was created by God, it is not too far-fetched to suggest that

Left: The Mycenaean period of Greek history occured between 1600 BC and ca. 1100 BC. This period of history is named after Mycenae, which was a military stronghold and significant area of civilization. Here is the Lion Gate of Mycenae. This gate is named for the sculptures of the two lionesses that guard the gate. Inset is the cover of the *Illustrated London News* from February 3, 1877, which featured Schliemann's excavations at Mycenae.

> The Bible makes it clear that the nation of Israel plays a central role in the history of the world.

we might witness the same kinds of skills emerging in all parts of the world. Some of the expressions of those skills would look different due to differences in environment, but there would be much similarity in their core substance.

THE UNIQUENESS OF ISRAEL

Standing in the middle of these world developments was the nation of Israel. The Bible makes it clear that the nation of Israel plays a central role in the history of the world. Thus, its establishment and purpose are important to note when we look at history.

Background

When God called Abram to leave his home and form the new nation of Israel, He did so to provide a path for blessing for all nations (Genesis 12:1–4). God formed this nation to be the path through which He would fully reveal Himself and bring the ultimate truth and salvation to the world (John 1:1–14;

Abraham prepares to sacrifice Isaac.
Original artist and date unknown.

Hebrews 1:1–2). Therefore, the nation of Israel was to be different from the surrounding nations. Their understanding of God was to be based on the character of Yahweh and His revealed law, which would lead them to be governed by a different moral foundation than that of other nations.

Yet when Abraham's descendants entered the promised land, they did not fully embrace this call and instead began to adopt the practices of the nations around them, spurning the law that had been given to them by God. They hid the light of truth under a bushel. When Israel acquiesced to the practices of the Canaanites, they blunted their purpose in world history. Even so, none of this stopped God from using Israel, though the path they traveled down was very rocky, to say the least.

The Early Years

After Israel entered the promised land, they found themselves facing a very strong force called the Philistines. The origins of the Philistines, who occupied the southern coast of Canaan, have been debated among scholars. It is theorized that the latter Philistines originated among the "sea peoples." Modern archaeology has also suggested early cultural links with the Mycenaean culture in Greece. The Philistines were most likely from the island of Crete and migrated to Canaan after the fall of the Mycenaean civilization. They were known for their fierce fighting, and later their name became associated with crude and uncivilized behavior. Eventually, the Greeks and Romans referred to the entire region of Israel by the name *Palestine*, which is a variant spelling of *Philistine*.

Because the Israelites refused to follow God in the manner that He had commanded them before they entered the land (Deuteronomy 6), He allowed them to struggle with the Philistines and other enemies. The Philistines were a tool in the hand of God to show Israel their sin and lead them to repentance. In the course of this struggle, God allowed leaders, or judges, to emerge in Israel to protect them from the worst of all outcomes.

One of the more familiar stories from the time of the judges is the story of Samson and Delilah (Judges 16), which has at its core the conflict between two nations: the people of Israel and the Philistines. As the Philistines waged war against Israel, God raised up Samson to help His people through divinely given strength.

Artists' renditions of Samson and Delilah have appeared in Bibles since publishers began including pictures in books. Here are three classic images. Original publication dates or artist information is unavailable.

In Judges 13, we read that the Israelites were turned over to the Philistines for forty years as a form of judgment for participating in the idolatry of the local people. This meant that the Philistines had a strong presence in the nation, and the people could not break free from Philistine control over their cities. This is what finally led the Israelites to seek an

For more details on the Philistines, read Judges.

earthly king. Though God was already their true King, the people were convinced that they needed an earthly king to enable them to stand firm against the Philistines and live in peace throughout the land.

God Grants Israel a King

Though the people's demand for a king was in certain respects an affront to God's rule as their ultimate King, God granted them their desire. The king

they were given, however, was one after *their* own heart, and thus they got Saul. Saul was a mighty man who was able to defend the nation from the Ammonites, and he demonstrated some success over the Philistines as well. But because Saul was disobedient to God, the kingdom was taken away from him and given to a man named David.

IMMEDIATELY AFTER DAVID WAS ANOINTED KING, BUT BEFORE HE HAD BEEN GIVEN THE THRONE, ONE OF THE MOST FAMILIAR EVENTS IN THE BIBLE OCCURRED: DAVID KILLED GOLIATH (1 SAMUEL 17). GOLIATH WAS LIKE A HUMAN TANK ON THE BATTLEFIELD: BIG, STRONG, DEADLY, AND SEEMINGLY INVULNERABLE. BECAUSE MOST COMBAT WAS HAND-TO-HAND, HIS IMMENSE HEIGHT AND REACH MADE HIM ALMOST INVIN-CIBLE. YET DAVID KILLED HIM AND SENT THE REST OF THE PHILISTINES FLEEING FOR THEIR LIVES. THIS ASTOUNDING VICTORY COULD ONLY HAVE BEEN ACCOMPLISHED BY GOD'S MAN, AND IT MARKED THE START OF THE ISRAELITES' LONG PROCESS OF DRIVING BACK THE PHILISTINES AND ESTABLISHING PEACE AND SECURITY IN THE PROMISED LAND.

Although the people of Israel often sinned against God and forfeited the blessings they could have gained by obedience, God did not stop declaring His truth through them or stop using this nation for His purposes. In raising

Michelangelo's *David*

up David, God put into place a leader who reflected His heart and His passion and brought together a nation that had been divided. The key to David's reign in Israel is that he sought to bring the honor, worship, and glory of God to the forefront (2 Samuel 6). Through David, we learn something very important about the purpose of history. In fact, through David, we learn a little more about where God is taking history. In 2 Samuel 7, God lays out for David and the world what He will bring about through his descendants.

God's Plan for Israel

After David ascended to the throne, he captured Jerusalem, established it as the capital of Israel, and moved the sacred ark of the covenant there. Then he made plans to build a huge and glorious temple where the ark could be placed. David's heart was to see that God was truly glorified, but God told David that this was not part of His plan. Instead, God had something better. Rather than have David build a house, or temple, for God, God was going to build David's "house" through his descendants—ultimately, Jesus.

An artist's interpretation of the ark of the covenant

■ *"And your house and your kingdom shall be made sure forever before me. Your throne shall be established forever* (2 Samuel 7:16).

God's plan was to establish the line of David as the perpetual rulers of Israel. Furthermore, God would protect the line of David so that eventually someone would come and reign on this throne forever. No other king or world leader will ever have ultimate control over the world. Only the throne of David has an eternal purpose. Psalm 2 highlights this amazing truth and the futility of those who struggle to gain power for themselves:

■ *Why do the nations rage and the peoples plot in vain? The kings of the earth set themselves, and the rulers take counsel together, against the* Lord *and against his*

Anointed, saying, "Let us burst their bonds apart and cast away their cords from us." He who sits in the heavens laughs; the Lord holds them in derision. Then he will speak to them in his wrath, and terrify them in his fury, saying, "As for me, I have set my King on Zion, my holy hill." I will tell of the decree: The LORD said to me, "You are my Son; today I have begotten you. Ask of me, and I will make the nations your heritage, and the ends of the earth your possession. You shall break them with a rod of iron and dash them in pieces like a potter's vessel." Now therefore, O kings, be wise; be warned, O rulers of the earth. Serve the LORD with fear, and rejoice with trembling. Kiss the Son, lest he be angry, and you perish in the way, for his wrath is quickly kindled. Blessed are all who take refuge in him (Psalm 2:1–12).

REFLECTIONS

The establishment of David's throne and eternal dynasty is an essential moment in the history of the world because it gives us some insight into the very heart and plan of God. God understands that nations will constantly struggle to gain more power than He has planned for them to have; yet God in heaven laughs, because He knows the futility of their struggles. He knows that there is no way for the kings of worldly nations to achieve their goals, because He has already picked the One who will rule the entire world. No king will ever get the full range of power and control he desires.

This doesn't mean that God does not allow kingdoms to have *any* power. God is the One who has given us governments, and they serve a purpose (Romans 13). Governments have been established by God to protect and care for the citizens of the state, and it is the duty of everyone to submit to the government. Yet Psalm 2 teaches that when kings or leaders seek to leave the bounds that God has established and seek ultimate power, they will never achieve it, because God has already appointed His King to rule the world. The kings of the world would be far better off paying homage to God's King lest they face His judgment.

In light of all of this, we should find a level of confidence. As nations emerge and rage against other nations, we should take hope that God will never allow any kingdom to achieve complete world dominance. We should also take hope that God has allowed the world to advance technologically, because He is kind and lets the rain fall on both the just and the unjust. Therefore, let us take hope in the power of our God and the promise that history is moving toward the establishment of His King.

TIME LINE
1500 BC – 1000 BC

BIBLE EVENT   WORLD EVENT

1500

1446—The Exodus; crossing of the Red Sea
1446–1406—Hebrews wander in the wilderness; God gives the Ten Commandments; building of the tabernacle

1406—Death of Moses; Joshua leads the Hebrews in their conquest of Canaan

1350—The first judges; the Hebrew people begin their struggle with the Philistines

Judges lead the Hebrews:
Othniel	Jair
Ehud	Jephthah
Shamgar	Ibzan
Deborah	Elon
Gideon	Abdon
Tola	Samson

1400

1300

1200

1100—Eli becomes a priest and judge

1060–1020—The ministry of Samuel
1051—Saul becomes king

1100

1011—David becomes king

1000

1500—The Aryans invade India
1500—The Lydians occupy Mycenae

1400—The creation of the cuneiform tablets in the royal library and temple of Ugarit

1372—Reign of Pharaoh Amenhotep (aka Ikhnato
1360—King Tut begins reign in Egypt

1304—Rameses II begins reign in Egypt
1300—Reign of Shalmaneser in Assyria

1200—The fall of the Hittite Empire and the beginning of the Iron Age
1190—The Trojan War

1100—Greece enters her Dark Ages
1100—Tiglath-Pileser I begins reign in Assyria

1050—Zhou dynasty begins in China
1050—Development of the Phoenician alphabet

1000—The Mayan Empire is founded in Central America

All dates are approximate.

CHAPTER 4

IMPACTS AND INTERSECTIONS

SACRED, SECULAR, AND REDEMPTIVE
1000–750 BC

History is a unique and fascinating field of study because it constantly draws us forward to the next great civilization or event. Everything that happens sets the stage for the next great event or movement in history. This journey is one that is filled with all kinds of ups and downs and twists and turns that offer new panoramic views of the world.

Every once in a while, things happen that have a lasting effect on later generations. Such is the nature of many of the events that took place in the time period covered in this chapter. This chapter surveys the people of Israel coming together as a nation, the advancements in China that continue to affect life and culture today, and the story behind the first Olympics.

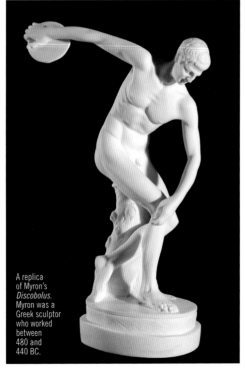

A replica of Myron's *Discobolus*. Myron was a Greek sculptor who worked between 480 and 440 BC.

As we study this period of history and observe these great turning points, we will again look from three points of view: *sacred*, *secular*, and *redemptive*. We will note shifts in world power, but not just to understand which powers ruled various parts of the world at this time. Rather, we will examine these power shifts to see how God interacted in the midst of them with the nation of Israel for His redemptive purposes. It was during this era that God allowed sacred, secular, and redemptive history to intersect in a very prominent way. This chapter takes us from the reign of David through the reign of Solomon and the construction of the temple in Israel to the division of the nation of Israel in a civil war. During this time, there were some powerful intersections of history that continue to affect our world today.

THE REIGN OF DAVID

David reigned as king over Israel from 1011 to 971 BC. David was an incredible man and a great leader—a man who really loved God and was chosen by Him to lead His people. He was a great warrior, an inspiring leader, a skilled musician, and a gifted composer of poetry and psalms. After David ascended to the throne, the nation of Israel and the people of the world were never the same. His life, humility, successes, failures, repentance, and faith have challenged the lives of millions of people for thousands of years.

Under the reign of David, the city of Jerusalem was captured from the Jebusites and became the capital of the nation. The Bible sometimes calls Jerusalem the City of David,

THE EXTENT OF DAVID'S KINGDOM

Extent of David's kingdom at the start of his reign

Extent of David's kingdom at the end of his reign

Territory added to Solomon's kingdom during his reign

0 20 40 60 80 100 mi
0 25 50 75 100 125 150 km

Left: Stained glass of King David. Original location and artist unknown. Above: Map of Israel during David's time.

but this refers to the portion of Jerusalem that David originally conquered, not the city as it is known today (see map on previous page). David then expanded the borders of the nation, making it strong and secure against neighboring powers.

At this time in history, a combination of international political factors brought Israel some respite from conflict with both Egypt and Assyria, the two greatest powers in the Near East.

By advancing far to the south and conquering Edom and the copper- and iron-rich Arabah Desert, David secured Israel's economic viability. Access to these natural resources enabled David to produce weaponry that helped him maintain power over the Philistines (1 Chronicles 22:1–3).

Having access to the Arabah region also gave David a strong base upon which to move north and secure the northern borders of Israel. Just to the north of Israel, in Syria, was a tribe of people called the Aramaeans. About this time, they were expanding into Mesopotamia and coming into conflict with the Assyrians there. Though the Assyrians themselves were emerging as a powerful force in the world, the Aramaeans acted as a thorn in their side, attacking them from time to time and holding them at bay. As David moved north, he conquered the Aramaean king Hadadezer (1 Chronicles 18:3).

AT THIS TIME IN HISTORY, A COMBINATION OF INTERNATIONAL POLITICAL FACTORS BROUGHT ISRAEL SOME RESPITE FROM CONFLICT WITH BOTH EGYPT AND ASSYRIA, THE TWO GREATEST POWERS IN THE NEAR EAST. AS THE NATION OF ISRAEL WAS CONSOLIDATED UNDER KING DAVID, EGYPT WAS PREOCCUPIED BY A CIVIL WAR BETWEEN UPPER EGYPT (IN THE SOUTH) AND LOWER EGYPT (IN THE NORTH). LOWER EGYPT WAS RULED BY THE PHARAOHS OF THE TWENTY-FIRST DYNASTY, AND UPPER EGYPT WAS RULED BY THE HIGH PRIESTS OF AMUN, WHO HIRED LIBYAN MERCENARIES TO SUPPORT THEIR RULE. ASSYRIA, AS NOTED EARLIER, WAS BEING KEPT AT BAY BY THE ARAMAEANS, A WANDERING GROUP OF NOMADS THAT EVENTUALLY SETTLED DOWN IN THE REGION NORTH OF ISRAEL. DAMASCUS WAS THE CAPITAL CITY OF THEIR KINGDOM.

With the major powers of the Near East effectively neutralized, David was able to unify the people of Israel and conquer some of the smaller nations in the surrounding area. David then desired to build a temple for the Lord, to replace the aging, portable tabernacle. Before David began the work, however, the Lord told him that this was not part of His plan.

For more on David's battles, read 1 Chronicles 11–20.

Instead, God was going to build David's house, meaning his dynasty, to rule over Israel forever (2 Samuel 7). This is another prophecy about the coming of the Messiah: He would be a descendant of David (Matthew 1:1; Romans 1:3; 2 Timothy 2:8). Through this single promise, God was clearly working in secular history, sacred history, and redemptive history all at once.

King Tang of Shang dynasty as imagined by Song dynasty painter Ma Lin

A BRIEF LOOK AT CHINA

In China, far to the east of Israel, very important developments were taking place that greatly affected the history of that nation. These events preoccupied the nation of China with matters that kept it from having a direct impact on sacred history.

During the reign of David in Israel, the Zhou dynasty in China usurped the throne from the Shang dynasty and eventually became the longest-reigning dynasty in the country's history.

In studying the history of China, Susan Wise Bauer has noted that "there were as yet no barbarians invading civilized people, no struggle between one nation and another. The greatest struggle was between a king's virtue and his wickedness. The threat to his throne came first from his own nature."*

*Susan Wise Bauer, *The History of the Ancient World* (New York: Norton, 2007), 164.

In short, China grew and developed without much contact or influence from other nations for a great many years. Rather than focusing on world domination, the Chinese kept an eye on their inward moral development, as characterized by the moral virtue of the king. If he became corrupted and perverted, then his kingdom would be usurped by a more virtuous king. This inward focus allowed the nation to develop a more isolated political culture.

Map of the Shang dynasty. The river running through the middle of the green-outlined area is the Yellow River.

The Shang dynasty began in roughly 1766 BC. This dynasty was called the Yellow River civilization because its cities were built around the eastern parts of the Yellow River. It was during this dynasty that the Bronze Age came to life in China. Bronze had been used in China before this dynasty, but it became much more integrated into daily Chinese life during this time.

The work of the Shang bronze craftsmen produced some of the greatest

Top left: This ax was used in hand-to-hand combat and was also a ritual object symbolizing power and military authority. The tomb it came from likely belonged to a man of wealth and influence. Top right: This bronze vessel is in the shape of a bat and was removed from the tomb of Lady Fu Hao, who lived during the Chinese Shang dynasty, thirteenth century BC.
Bottom left: This is a vessel with a zigzag thunder pattern from the early Zhou period. Bottom right: A ritual vessel on a pedestal, used as a container for grain. From the Western Zhou dynasty, dated around 1000 BC. The written inscription of eleven ancient Chinese characters on the bronze vessel states its use and ownership by Zhou royalty.

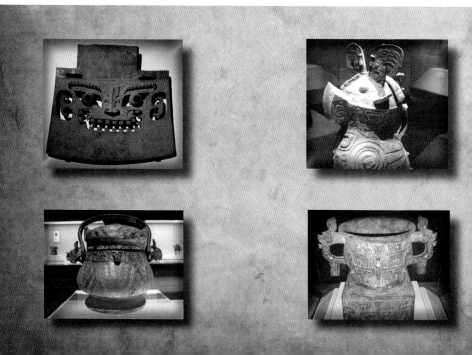

bronze work in history. No other nation was able to form such complex and sophisticated designs in bronze. Also, by the time of the Shang dynasty, the Chinese alphabet had developed and evolved into the form and structure used today.

The advancement that writing made in China under the Shang dynasty brought about a fascinating religious movement as well. Once the ideograms became sophisticated enough for communicating well, they were used to seek the divine spirits to find answers to life's questions. In the ruins of the Shang capital, archaeologists have discovered hundreds of bones with Chinese characters engraved on them. These bones, now called *oracle bones*, were used to seek answers from the divine, sometimes even from family members who had died and who were believed to be in heaven guiding those still on earth.

If someone had a question, they would visit a priest at the temple. These priests would apply heat to a dried bone or turtle shell until the surface cracked. Then the priest would read the crack much like someone today might try to find guidance from reading a palm or tarot cards. The message from these bones or shells was believed to be divine.

The demise of the Shang dynasty began during the reign of Wu-yi, who ruled for about seventy-seven years before the Shang dynasty fell. He was a corrupt king whose main offense to the people was that he showed disrespect to the gods. Wu-yi cast lots (something like dice or playing cards today), and if certain combinations that were regarded as favorable omens turned up in his favor, he mocked the gods as lousy gamblers. Such disrespect for the gods was regarded by the people as a serious moral failure and a violation of Wu-yi's responsibility as king.

Oracle Bones

Top: Oracle bone with the earliest Chinese characters

Middle: Oracle bones from the Shang dynasty

Bottom: Replica of an oracle turtle shell with ancient Chinese oracle scripts inscribed on it

Painting of Wu completed in the seventh century by Yen Li-Pen. It is part of a larger work entitled *Thirteen Emperors Scroll.*

As the oracle bone ritual became more and more integrated into Chinese life, it increased the role of the king as head of the courts. The seeking of wisdom from the courts through the use of communication with the divine united the institutions of government and religion. Therefore, a king who mocked the gods became anathema. For this reason, when Wu-yi was struck by lightning while out hunting, many believed this to be the act of the gods punishing the king for his rebellion. He was succeeded by his son and then his grandson, both of whom, according to Chinese history, continued the moral decline started by Wu-yi.

Wu-yi's great-grandson, Chou, was the worst king of all Wu-yi's descendants. Chou was a gifted man who was praised for his strength, intelligence, oratory skills, and perception. Unfortunately, he used all these skills for debauchery. His life was bent upon wine, pleasure, and immoral relationships with women. He raised taxes to finance his licentious lifestyle. His depravity quickly turned to political tyranny. He demanded complete loyalty to himself. Anyone suspected of disloyalty to his reign was forced to lie on burning hot rocks.

Eventually, however, the wicked ways of Chou and his ancestors appear to have caught up with them, for they were attacked by a neighboring tribe, the Zhou, who lived just to the west of the people of the Shang dynasty. Under the leadership of a king named Wen, who was regarded as faithful to

A hanging silk scroll of King Wu of the Zhou dynasty. On display at the National Palace Museum in Taipei.

the moral ways of heaven, and his son Wu, the Zhou were successful in overthrowing the Shang dynasty.

When Wu conquered the Shang dynasty, he did so with brute force. This offended many in China, for they saw it as a violation of the integrity of the king. Therefore, Wu had to work hard to justify his position as king. At the start of his reign, Wu offered sacrifices to the gods to make up for his perceived sins, and then set aside all the weapons of war that he had amassed for the battle. This act helped to maintain the support of the people and the authority of his throne.

After Wu died, his young son, Ch'eng, became king, though initially the country was ruled by a regent, due to Ch'eng's youthfulness. One of Ch'eng's more significant contributions to Chinese culture—which still exists today— was a religio-political concept called the Mandate of Heaven. Ch'eng defined the kingship as an intermediary position between heaven and earth, thus establishing the king as the one divinely approved to rule the people. This mandate gave the king divine authority to act for the good of the nation. The Chinese character for emperor or lord, *wang*, demonstrates this eloquently.

The symbol consists of three horizontal lines joined by a vertical line. This character represents the connection between heaven (the top line) and earth (the bottom line) with the king in between (the middle line).

The theology behind the mandate is that heaven desires that humans be provided for in all their needs, and the emperor is appointed by heaven to see to the people's welfare. If the emperor, or king, having fallen into selfishness and corruption, fails to see to the welfare of the people, heaven withdraws its mandate and invests it in another. The only way to know that the mandate had passed was by an attempt to overthrow the king or emperor; if the coup succeeded, it meant the mandate had passed to another. If it failed, the mandate still resided with the king.

THE MANDATE OF HEAVEN IS PROBABLY THE MOST CRITICAL SOCIAL AND POLITICAL CONCEPT IN CHINESE CULTURE. IT HAS AFFECTED HISTORICAL CHANGE AND PROVIDED A PROFOUND MORAL THEORY OF GOVERNMENT BASED ON THE SELFLESS DEDICATION OF THE RULER TO THE BENEFIT OF THE GENERAL POPULATION. THE CONCEPT ALSO RECREATES THE CHINESE CONCEPT OF HEAVEN, WHICH WAS DERIVED FROM THE EARLIER CONCEPT OF A "LORD ON HIGH" OR "SHANG-TI," INTO A FORCE THAT REGULATES THE MORAL UNIVERSE. THIS MORAL ASPECT OF HEAVEN, ALONG WITH THE MANDATE OF HEAVEN, INFLU-ENCED CHINESE CULTURE AND PHILOSOPHY TO FOCUS ON MORAL AND SOCIAL ISSUES MORE SO THAN PERHAPS ANY OTHER ANCIENT CULTURE.

SOLOMON: THE PROSPEROUS INTERNATIONAL

Returning to the history of Israel: After King David died, his son Solomon became king, establishing the new precedent of dynastic succession for Israel's kings. Solomon was clearly a different type of king than David. David was a passionate fighter who inspired others to follow him. Solomon was a builder and a very impressive manager. Under Solomon, the nation was reorganized into twelve administrative districts. He also reworked the tax system and began work on the temple, one of the greatest building programs in the history of ancient Israel. This temple was forty-five feet high, constructed of quarried stone, lined with carved cedar, coated with gold, and filled with incredible treasures.

Presents to King Solomon. A miniature from the Georgian Jruchi Gospels (fifteenth century).

Solomon had a reputation not only for being a master builder and an incredibly wealthy man (his stables boasted twelve thousand horses) but also for his wisdom. This reputation existed well beyond the borders of Israel; on one occasion, the queen of Sheba came to Solomon to test his famed wisdom (1 Kings 10). Sheba was probably located somewhere around modern-day Ethiopia. The

The Islamic Dome of the Rock and Jewish Wailing Wall in modern-day Jerusalem. Both are located near the site of the original temple, which was conceived by King David but built by his son, King Solomon.

queen of Sheba's arrival in Israel demonstrates how extensive international trade had become by this time. When she arrived, she brought with her many goods to share with Solomon.

For more
on the
queen of Sheba,
read
1 Kings 10.

■ *Then she gave the king 120 talents of gold, and a very great quantity of spices and precious stones. Never again came such an abundance of spices as these that the queen of Sheba gave to King Solomon. Moreover, the fleet of Hiram, which brought gold from Ophir, brought from Ophir a very great amount of almug wood and precious stones (1 Kings 10:10–11).*

Solomon and Sheba by Konrad Witz (1435)

Solomon's international ventures involved more than just Sheba; he also developed important relationships with Tyre and Egypt. Solomon established a mutually lucrative alliance with Hiram, the king of Tyre. Hiram supplied Solomon with cedar and pine from Lebanon, as well as with skilled artisans for his building projects. Tyrian sailors were also drafted into Solomon's navy, because the Israelites were not experienced at sea (1 Kings 9:26–27), and Phoenician ships sailed along with those from Israel. In return, Hiram received access to the Red Sea, as well as large supplies of wheat, barley, wine, and oil from the land of Israel (1 Kings 5:11; 2 Chronicles 2:10). At the conclusion of the great palace and temple building projects, which occupied twenty years, Solomon presented Hiram with twenty villages (1 Kings 9:11; 2 Chronicles 8:2), and Hiram gave Solomon a large amount of gold (1 Kings 9:14).

Phoenician ship carved on the face of a sarcophagus. Second century AD.

Solomon also married the daughter of the Egyptian pharaoh, likely sealing an alliance with Egypt. Pharaoh gave Solomon the town of Gezer as a dowry (1 Kings 9:16). Though this marriage and alliance are rightly understood as indicators of Solomon's great wealth and political power, they were not seen by the writers of scripture as a positive advancement for Israel. God had forbidden these relationships in the laws of Moses because they would draw the heart of the king away from God, which is precisely what happened.

■ *Now King Solomon loved many foreign women, along with the daughter of Pharaoh: Moabite, Ammonite, Edomite, Sidonian, and Hittite women, from the nations concerning which the LORD had said to the people of Israel, "You shall not enter into marriage with them, neither shall they with you, for surely they will turn away your heart after their gods." Solomon clung to these in love. He had 700 wives, princesses, and 300 concubines. And his wives turned away his heart.*

For when Solomon was old his wives turned away his heart after other gods, and his heart was not wholly true to the LORD his God, as was the heart of David his father. For Solomon went after Ashtoreth the goddess of the Sidonians, and after Milcom the abomination of the Ammonites (1 Kings 11:1–5).

Solomon's Sin, as in 1 Kings 11:4–13. Illustration from a Bible card published in 1896 by the Providence Lithograph Company.

Solomon's international relationships transformed Israel into a much more cosmopolitan nation. Ultimately, Solomon became a study in contrasts. On the one hand, he built a great temple for the glory of God; on the other, he pursued the pleasures of the world with near abandon. Yet Solomon's accomplishments and experiences also enabled him to pass on great wisdom about life:

■ *Remember also your Creator in the days of your youth, before the evil days come and the years draw near of which you will say, "I have no pleasure in them"; before the sun and the light and the moon and the stars are darkened and the clouds return after the rain, in the day when the keepers of the house tremble, and the strong men are bent, and the grinders cease because they are few, and those who look through the windows are dimmed, and the doors on the street are shut—*

when the sound of the grinding is low, and one rises up at the sound of a bird, and all the daughters of song are brought low—they are afraid also of what is high, and terrors are in the way; the almond tree blossoms, the grasshopper drags itself along, and desire fails, because man is going to his eternal home, and the mourners go about the streets—before the silver cord is snapped, or the golden bowl is broken, or the pitcher is shattered at the fountain, or the wheel broken at the cistern, and the dust returns to the earth as it was, and the spirit returns to God who gave it. Vanity of vanities, says the Preacher; all is vanity (Ecclesiastes 12:1–8).

It is important to take a moment to learn a lesson from King Solomon and his life. Through Solomon, we learn that life is temporal. A person might have access to everything this world can offer; but in the end, everything outside a relationship with God is vanity. Happiness cannot be found in power, pleasure, or riches. Through Solomon, we learn that the most important aspect of life is to reverently serve the God of all history, who is the source of life and meaning that we all truly long for. Those who seek meaning in power, possessions, pleasure, and riches will come up empty in the end.

THE DIVIDED KINGDOM: A TIME OF WAR

It appears that Solomon's international alliances and many building projects created strong tensions in Israel that eventually led to the division of the nation. Consider what it took to build Solomon's magnificent temple. He conscripted thirty thousand Israelite men as laborers in the building project, sending them away to work in Lebanon one out of every three months (1 Kings 5:13–14). Even though these men were paid for their labor, they were nonetheless forced into the work. In addition to building the temple, they also had to keep their own fields and vines and care for their

> **For more on the divided kingdom, read 2 Chronicles 10.**

own families. Add to this the responsibility that each of the twelve districts had to maintain and support Solomon's administration and royal court, which included the king's hundreds of wives. It is easy to see that this must have been a heavy burden for the nation to bear. There is no doubt that even in Solomon's time, cracks were beginning to show that would eventually lead to the division of the nation.

After Solomon died and his son Rehoboam took the throne, the northern tribes of Israel demanded that he lighten the burden they were required to

Hans Holbein the younger began working on the murals for the Council Chamber of Basel Town Hall during the 1520s, painting classical subjects. After his return from a two-year visit to England (1526–1528), he was commissioned to resume the task, but this time to provide murals based on Old Testament subjects, in keeping with the new Reformation doctrines of the authorities. The murals were one of several large-scale projects undertaken by Holbein that are now known only from a few fragments and preparatory sketches. This design portrays Rehoboam, the son of Solomon, whose arrogant government led to his people's rebellion and the loss of part of his kingdom. He holds out his little finger, saying, "My little finger is thicker than my father's waist!" The murals reminded the councillors of the need for wise and godly government.

bear for the government. Rehoboam foolishly refused and threatened even greater burdens for the people. The northern tribes reacted by rebelling and setting up their own king named Jeroboam, a former official of Solomon's court. Rehoboam now ruled over only Judah and Benjamin in the south; all the other tribes joined the northern kingdom.

Around this same time, the nation of Egypt was briefly reunified. This allowed Sheshonq (or Shishak, as the Bible calls him), the new pharaoh, to recapture lost territory. He even advanced on Jerusalem and attacked the city.

In the fifth year of King Rehoboam, Shishak king of Egypt came up against Jerusalem. He took away the treasures of the house of the LORD and the treasures of the king's house. He took away everything. He also took away all the shields of gold that Solomon had made, and King Rehoboam made in their place shields of bronze, and committed them to the hands of the officers of the guard, who kept the door of the king's house. And as often as the king went into the house of the LORD, the guard carried them and brought them back to the guardroom (1 Kings 14:25–28).

> Ahab married the king's daughter, Jezebel. This union eventually brought God's judgment on Israel.

Also at this time, Assyrians, under King Ashur-dan II, were finally able to push back the Aramaeans, thus reestablishing their power and reviving their country. This event brought Assyria out of its Dark Ages and into what historians call the Assyrian Renaissance.

Several generations later, Shalmaneser III became king of Assyria. He continued to solidify his strength in the region and began to advance toward the northern kingdom of Israel. Ahab was king of Israel during this time, and he sought to strengthen the nation by developing an alliance with the Phoenician king of the city of Sidon. Apparently in order to seal the alliance, Ahab married the king's daughter, Jezebel. This union eventually brought God's judgment on Israel.

Jezebel's wickedness has become proverbial, but few people realize that her coming to Israel, and hence the trouble that followed, was the direct result of Ahab's failure to trust and obey God. Through his marriage to Jezebel, Ahab sought to strengthen himself against the Assyrians; but God had

Left: The relief of Sheshonq I's campaign list at the southern exterior walls of the temple of Karnak, north of Luxor, Egypt. Above: Basalt statue of King Shalmaneser III, 858–824 BC (Neo-Assyrian period). Found in Assur (Qal'at Sharqat). Today it is displayed in the Istanbul Archaeological Museums, in the Museum of the Ancient Orient section. The following text is from a display at this statue, a translation of script on the actual statue: "Shalmaneser, the great king, the mighty king, king of all the four regions, the powerful and the mighty rival of the princes of the whole universe, the great ones, the kings, son of Assur-Nairapli, king of universe, king of Assyria, grandson of Tukulti-Ninurta, king of universe, king of Assyria." The inscription continues by describing his campaigns and deeds of the lands of Urartu, Syria, Namri, Que, and Tabal, and ends with this: "At that time I rebuilt the walls of my city Ashur from their foundations to their summits. I made an image of my royal self and set it up by the metalworkers' gate."

Top: *Elijah Denouncing Ahab* (original date and artist unknown). Bottom: *The Death of Jezebel* from Doré's English Bible. By Gustave Doré in 1866.

promised from the very beginning of the nation that He would care for them as long as they stayed devoted to Him (Joshua 1). Nevertheless, Ahab sought to take matters into his own hands and establish an alliance for protection apart from God.

When Ahab married Jezebel, he rejected God and began to worship Baal, the god worshipped in Sidon. Throughout Israel's history up to this point, various Israelites had added the worship of Baal to the worship of Yahweh, resulting in a wicked compromise. But Ahab's sin went even further in that he rejected Yahweh altogether in order to worship Baal. First Kings 16:29–33 gives a frightening description of Ahab's treachery:

■ *In the thirty-eighth year of Asa king of Judah, Ahab the son of Omri began to reign over Israel, and Ahab the son of Omri reigned over Israel in Samaria twenty-two years. And Ahab the son of Omri did evil in the sight of the* Lord, *more than all who were before him. And as if it had been a light thing for him to walk in the sins of Jeroboam the son of Nebat, he took for his wife Jezebel the daughter of Ethbaal king of the Sidonians, and went and served Baal and worshiped him. He erected an altar for Baal in the house of Baal, which he built in Samaria. And Ahab made an Asherah. Ahab did more to provoke the* Lord, *the God of Israel, to anger than all the kings of Israel who were before him.*

Despite Ahab's attempts to present a formidable front against the Aramaeans, the king of Damascus gathered thirty-two Aramaean warlords and mounted an attack on Israel (1 Kings 20). Despite this enormous, combined force arrayed against Israel, God protected His people, and the battle was fought to a draw. A treaty was then established that kept peace between the Aramaeans and the Israelites for many years.

GREECE

We must pause for a moment in our story about Israel and look at some important developments that were taking place at the same time in Greece. These developments later became very important to sacred history. For us to fully comprehend what was going on in Greece, a little context is necessary.

Zeus in Olympia. Phidias's statue in gold and ivory in Olympia's main temple. The statue was twelve meters high and decorated with paintings and precious stones.

At this point in history, Greece was not a unified country but was instead divided into many autonomous city-states. These city-states often battled each other, and many had differing forms of government. The city-state of Sparta, for example, was ruled by a dual kingship, governed by two hereditary kings of the Agiad and Eurypontids families. Both men were supposedly descendants of Heracles (the mythic Greek hero and son of Zeus) and equal in authority, so that one could not act against the veto of the other.

Ruins of old pillars, Olympia, Greece

Many of the other Greek city-states were ruled by more traditional aristocratic governments—generally a small elite class of rulers, with commoners having little or no power.

> The Greeks believed that the Pythia was the spokeswoman of the sun god Apollo, who in turn communicated the will of his father, Zeus.

Some years later in Greek history, another form of government—called democracy—emerged in Athens. We will examine this development in greater detail in chapter 5. For now, we will simply note that in a democracy, the people rule by either directly voting on issues or electing someone to operate on their behalf.

By early 700 BC, the Greek city of Olympia was growing in size. It had been a religious center for centuries, with the worship of Hera and Zeus drawing people there from all over Greece. As people from the various city-states migrated to Olympia to worship, some seeds of unity among them were planted.

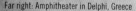

Top: The Temple of Apollo at Delphi, Greece

Top right: A row of shops from the Roman period at Delphi. The shops originally stood along the back of a colonnade (stoa). This small agora (marketplace) stood near the entrance to the sacred way leading up to the Temple of Apollo. Among other things, the shops would have sold votive objects and figurines that devotees could offer to the deity when they came seeking advice from the Delphic oracle. The remains of the temple are visible in the distance, farther up the slope, where four thick pillars still stand.

Middle right: Part of the starting line at the stadium at Olympia

Bottom right: The Treasury of Athens, the most complete building at the site of Delphi, holiest of ancient Greek sites, the site of the Pythian Games and of the Delphic oracle. The treasury was built by the Athenians to commemorate (and with the spoils of) the Battle of Marathon.

Far right: Amphitheater in Delphi, Greece

Similarly, a little farther north of Olympia, another temple was built in the city of Delphi. In this temple, an oracle could be sought from a priest or priestess. The oracle at Delphi was one of the more influential and powerful Greek institutions; thus, through this temple, another seed for unity was planted.

Individuals and government leaders came to Delphi to pose questions regarding every kind of problem, both personal and political. To answer these questions, the high priestess, called the Pythia, uttered prophecies while in a state of frenzy. The Greeks believed that the Pythia was the spokeswoman of the sun god Apollo, who in turn communicated the will of his father, Zeus, through the Pythia. As the voice of Apollo and Zeus, the Pythia could set government policies, cause cities to be built and colonies to be established, and begin or end wars.

It is interesting to note that Olympia itself was influenced by the oracle at Delphi. According to tradition, the famous Olympic Games were first instituted because of a Delphic oracle given to the king of Elis, a small city near

Olympia. The king's hope was that the Games would bring an end to the many conflicts between the Greek city-states. These Games were to be held every four years, during a monthlong truce between the city-states. This truce was eventually extended to three months to allow safe passage for all the participants. The Games never brought about the peace that Elis had longed for, but there was a great time of unity during the Games.

Alexander the Great in battle. This mosaic was created in the second half of the second century BC.

The seeds of unity planted during this time would not bear their full fruit until the rise of Alexander the Great. Through Alexander, Greece emerged as a world empire that God used to advance both sacred and redemptive history.

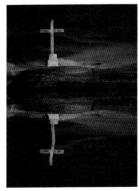

REFLECTIONS

One of the great things about studying history is the opportunity it affords to see the movements of the world from different perspectives. As noted before, God is the God of all history. Thus, we see His hand moving and shaping sacred and secular history for a single purpose: to bring about His redemptive work. As one nation rises up against another, it seems arbitrary—until God speaks. And then we see why God has allowed it to happen.

By properly considering history from these distinct perspectives, we can see a fuller picture of God at work in the great movements of history. When we discern the great intersections of sacred, secular, and redemptive history, we experience a great leap in our overall understanding of history. Whether we are talking about David (and the events of the world that allowed him to secure the nation and receive the promise of an eternal kingdom) or Solomon (who rose to become a preeminent world leader only to teach us that outside of the purposes of God nothing brings true meaning in this world), when sacred, secular, and redemptive history intersect, our understanding of history is illuminated with new, vibrant color and beauty.

TIME LINE
1000 BC – 750 BC

BIBLE EVENT   **WORLD EVENT**

1000

971—Solomon begins reign

931—The kingdom divides

NORTHERN KINGDOM
Dates when they begin reign

SOUTHERN KINGDOM
Dates when they begin reign

913—Abijah
911—Asa

910—Nadab
909—Baasha

886—Elah
885—Zimri and Tibni
885—Omri
874—Ahab
873—Ahaziah

852—Joram
841—Jehu

814—Jehoahaz

798—Jehoash
793—Jeroboam II

753—Zechariah
752—Shallum
752—Menahem

873—Jehoshaphat
853—Joram
842—Ahaziah
841—Athaliah
835—Joash

796—Amaziah
792—Uzziah

740—Jotham

Prophets
870—Elijah begins ministry
845—Elisha begins ministry
770—Jonah goes to Nineveh
760—Isaiah begins ministry
758—Hosea begins ministry
755—Amos begins ministry

900

800

700

978—Hiram begins reign in Tyre

945—Shishak I begins reign in Egypt; Egypt briefly unified again

858—Shalmaneser III begins reign in Assyria
850—Assyria pushes back the Aramaeans
841—Israel begins paying tribute to Assyria

800—Greek city-states begin to organize

783—Shalmaneser IV reigns in Assyria
776—First Olympic Games

753—Rome is founded; Romulus is king
750—Homer writes the *Iliad* in Greece

All dates are approximate.

CHAPTER 5

CAPTIVITY AND HOPE

TRANSITION AND CHANGE
750–500 BC

It has been said that change never hurt anyone, but transition kills. In other words, it's not the final product of change that is difficult for people; it is the process of transitioning from the old to the new. For example, it is not difficult to exchange an old car for a new one. What is difficult is to sacrifice all the espressos and mochas to save up money for the new car. On balance, this may be true, not just in our personal lives, but also in the grander scheme of history.

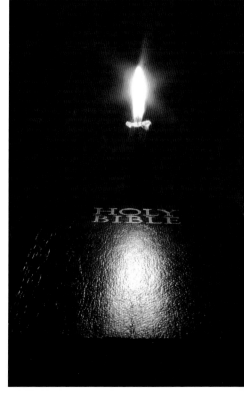

When we look at world history, we find that the many transitions from one nation's rise to another's are marked by a great deal of suffering. As power is wrested from one regime and put in the hands of another, the typical by-products are pain, suffering, and death. This is seen quite clearly in the events of history that are discussed in this chapter. This particular period, between 750 and 500 BC, was marked by massive shifts in world power, and every shift brought with it intense distress and affliction.

Yet this chapter is not a dismal record of suffering and death. We will also witness the God of history speaking and giving words of hope in the midst of these difficult times. The words He speaks fall like water in a desert. They are words of anticipation and great news, assuring His people that, even though the world was changing and shifting all around them, God was still at work accomplishing His purposes. Those who lived for His glory would experience great blessing.

This period is also especially fascinating because of the great overlap between secular, sacred, and redemptive history during this time.

A TIME OF WARNING
740–701 BC

"From unity to division to unity" could be a slogan that describes the history of Israel from the time of Samuel to the return of the Israelites from captivity. From the end of the book of Ruth to the early chapters of 1 Samuel, we read that Israel was in disarray. Then God appointed a man named Saul to be king, and after him God raised up David, who ruled over a strong, united nation.

ONLY TWO GENERATIONS AFTER DAVID, THIS POWERFUL NATION WAS SPLIT BY TWO RIVAL FACTIONS. HOWEVER, GOD WAS NOT DONE WITH THE PEOPLE OF ISRAEL; CENTURIES LATER, THROUGH THE HORRIBLE EXPERIENCE OF CAPTIVITY, THE NATION WAS AGAIN UNITED. THIS MOVEMENT FROM UNITY TO DIVISION TO UNITY OCCURRED DURING A TIME OF MASSIVE POLITICAL MOVEMENT IN THE WORLD, WHEN POWER SHIFTED FROM KINGDOM TO KINGDOM AND THE WORLD EXPERIENCED SOME VERY IMPORTANT DEVELOPMENTS THAT HAVE SHAPED EVEN OUR PRESENT AGE.

When Israel split into two nations (ca. 931 BC), the ten northern tribes became known as the northern kingdom, or simply Israel, and the tribes of Judah and Benjamin became known as the southern kingdom, or simply Judah. The first king over the northern tribes, Jeroboam I, did not want anyone in his kingdom to worship at the temple in Jerusalem, which was the capital of the southern kingdom. So he established pagan shrines at Dan and Bethel, and he encouraged the people to worship there instead.

Jeroboam used images of young bulls to represent the Lord—reminiscent of the golden calf idol built by the Israelites after the Exodus when they were waiting for Moses to return from the mountaintop (Exodus 32). This action by Jeroboam typified the northern kingdom's rejection of God's law and set the precedent for their continual rebellion against God.

A major consequence of their rebellion was that the leaders of the northern kingdom used their religion as a means of gaining an advantage over the people; therefore, they abused the powerless and took advantage of the weak. As we will soon see, God sent prophets to warn

This classic map was first published by the American Bible Society in 1888.

Israel that judgment was coming; if they did not repent of their ways, they would be dealt with severely. (See Amos 5 for a description of these practices.)

The Adoration of the Golden Calf painted by Nicolas Poussin between 1633 and 1636

The shrines that Jeroboam I established at Dan and Bethel (1 Kings 12:29), together with the people's openness in worshipping Baal, turned the northern kingdom into a society just as pagan as its neighbors. They began to regard Yahweh as simply one god among the many others they might worship.

Therefore, God raised up a prophet named Elijah to warn the Israelites to stop their false worship. Elijah confronted the prophets of Baal on Mount Carmel and showed the people that only God had true power and that to worship Baal was folly (1 Kings 18:21–24).

By 750 BC, the economic state of the northern kingdom looked very good, even while the religious and moral climates were abysmal. The rich got richer by taking advantage of the poor. Those in power exacted taxes from the poor and took away what little they had, in order to make themselves richer and to live in better homes (Amos 5). It seems the nation had fallen into a state of greed, unethical practices, and injustice.

Internationally, things were a bit unsettling as well, and this contributed to the abuses going on in Israel. Egypt was in a state of decline. Decades earlier (ca. 801 BC), the Assyrians had captured Damascus in Syria but were forced to withdraw due to problems in other regions of their empire. These international problems afforded Israel the opportunity to flour-

For more on God's warnings, see Amos 5.

ish and recover some of the territory it had lost to Aram. Israel increased in prosperity, but this did little more than increase the power of the abusers within the nation. Those who had no power were even more oppressed by the powerful as the wealth of the kingdom increased.

The northern kingdom at this time is a study in contrasts. On the one hand, they were prosperous, enjoying much economic success. On the other hand, they were very rebellious toward the law of God. Ever since Israel had split into two kingdoms, no godly leaders—like a Moses, Samuel, or David— had emerged to bring the nation back into union and obedience to God.

Left: Limestone carving of Baal with a thunderbolt. It was found at the acropolis in Ugarit.
Right: The dangerous cliffs of Mount Carmel.

Instead, they kept focusing on their own positions of power and prosperity, and they turned away from trusting God and walking in obedience to Him.

Sometime around 755 BC, God raised up a man named Amos as a prophetic voice to speak a word of warning to the northern kingdom. Amos was originally a shepherd from the Judean town of Tekoa, a few miles south of Bethlehem. Though he was not a professional prophet, God gave him an extraordinary message of warning for the northern kingdom.

AMOS MADE HIS WAY TO ISRAEL AND TOLD THEM THAT THEIR LOVE FOR MONEY, POWER, AND SUCCESS WAS A WRETCHED STENCH TO GOD. THEIR LOVE OF PERSONAL GAIN SO DOMINATED THEIR LIVES THAT THEY TOOK ADVANTAGE OF THE WEAK, DID NOT CARE FOR THE POOR, NEGLECTED JUSTICE, AND DID WHATEVER THEY WANTED AS LONG AS THEY PERSONALLY PROSPERED. "PREPARE TO MEET YOUR GOD" WAS AMOS'S MESSAGE (AMOS 4:12). FOR THE RICH WHO TOOK ADVANTAGE OF THE POOR, AMOS CALLED OUT, "LET JUSTICE ROLL DOWN LIKE WATERS" (5:24). HIS MESSAGE CALLED FOR RIGHTEOUSNESS—RIGHT WORSHIP THAT WOULD BRING ABOUT RIGHT ETHICS AND MORALITY FOR THE NATION.

Amos was joined by another prophet, named Hosea, who also brought a word from the Lord concerning Israel's rebellion. However, Hosea's message was different in that he was given a very strange task to perform: He was told to marry a prostitute, and each time she was unfaithful to him, he was to forgive her and take her back. The purpose behind this graphic commission was to illustrate to Israel that they were in rebellion, spiritually living the life of a harlot, but that God would not renege on His promise to the nation and would be faithful even when they were faithless. God wanted Israel to know that a path of restoration was waiting for them if they would only return to Him.

However, even though God would not go back on His promise to His people, He would also be faithful to His holiness and bring judgment to bear on the nation. This is why He raised up the Assyrians to conquer the northern kingdom around 721 BC. God had sent message after message to the leaders of Israel that they were going in the wrong direction. Throughout the north-

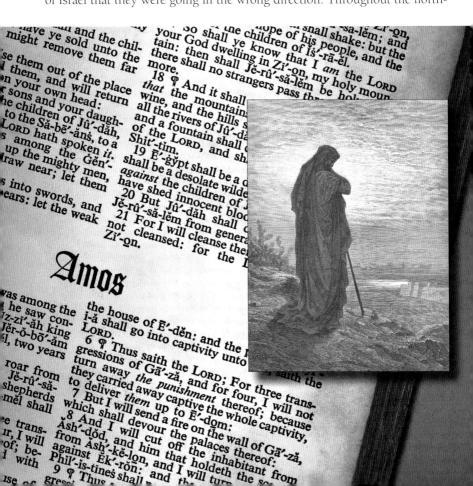

ern kingdom's history, twenty kings sat on the throne. Only one died a natural death; usurpers assassinated four others; and Hoshea, the final king, died in Assyrian captivity. Yet even this tumultuous turnover of leadership failed to bring the people to their senses and cause them to turn from their sin.

At this point, it will be helpful for us to take a moment to understand the Assyrian Empire better, to gain more perspective on its rise to power, and to see how it affected the northern kingdom of Israel.

THE ASSYRIAN EMPIRE AND THE NORTHERN KINGDOM OF ISRAEL

In order to comprehend the international tensions in the Near East at this time, it is important to understand some of the history of Assyria and the other nations of the region. Assyria was to the far north of Israel. Immediately southwest of Assyria was Syria, which was ruled by the Aramaeans. Just south of Syria was the northern kingdom of Israel, and just south of that was the southern kingdom of Judah.

Around the year 783 BC, Assyria was ruled by Shalmaneser IV, who ruled the nation for nine years. He was different from the previous kings of Assyria, most notably because he appeared to be less boastful. Kings of this era would typically boast of their past conquests and their anticipated

The Prophet Hosea

Left: Engraving by Gustave Doré (1832–1883). Top right: Statue of the prophet Hosea sculpted by Aleijadinho. This sculpture, which is made from soapstone, stands in Congonhas, Minas Gerais, Brazil. The artist lived between 1730 and 1814. Middle right: Prophet Hosea on the "Käthchenhaus" of Heilbronn, Germany, sixteenth century. Bottom right: *The Prophet Hosea* by Duccio di Buoninsegna as it appears in Siena Cathedral. Original art created in the early fourteenth century.

future conquests, often exaggerating their victories to appear more impressive than they really were. The inscriptions from Shalmaneser IV's rule, however, were notably subdued in their descriptions of his successes. One possible reason for his relatively humble attitude was that he ruled during a difficult time in Assyrian history. During his reign, the country faced pressure from the Aramaeans, as well as from some small tribes to the north called the Hurrians.

> ## Many historians believe that Jeroboam II could not have moved that far north without some acquiescence from Assyria.

It was also during this time that Jeroboam II began to expand the borders of Israel (2 Kings 14:23–27), capturing land far north into Syria. Many historians believe that Jeroboam II could not have moved that far north without some acquiescence from Assyria. Susan Wise Bauer posits that some sort of treaty was signed between Israel and Assyria.*

Jeroboam II, who ruled from 793 to 753 BC, reigned during the time of the prophet Jonah. During this time, God called Jonah to go to Nineveh (Assyria's capital) to preach a word of judgment to the Assyrians. It is very interesting to reflect on how God worked in this situation. He allowed Assyria to be in such a state of need, and Israel to be in such a state of strength, that Assyria would be reluctant to rebuff a prophet of Israel traveling about their capital city. This political situation opened the door for Jonah to come to this clearly pagan nation to warn them about an impending judgment. Observe what happened when Jonah arrived in Nineveh:

> ■ Now Nineveh was an exceedingly great city, three days' journey in breadth. Jonah began to go into the city, going a day's journey. And he called out, "Yet forty days, and Nineveh shall be overthrown!" And the

*Susan Wise Bauer, *The History of the Ancient World* (New York: Norton, 2007), 363.

people of Nineveh believed God. They called for a fast and put on sackcloth, from the greatest of them to the least of them. The word reached the king of Nineveh, and he arose from his throne, removed his robe, covered himself with sackcloth, and sat in ashes. And he issued a proclamation and published through Nineveh, "By the decree of the king and his nobles: Let neither man nor beast, herd nor flock, taste anything. Let them not feed or drink water, but let man and beast be covered with sackcloth, and let them call out mightily to God. Let everyone turn from his evil way and from the violence that is in his hands. Who knows? God may turn and relent and turn from his fierce anger, so that we may not perish." When God saw what they did, how they turned from their evil way, God relented of the disaster that he had said he would do to them, and he did not do it (Jonah 3:3–10).

> **For more on Jonah's visit to Nineveh, see Jonah 1–4.**

When Jonah preached his message to Nineveh, the Assyrian Empire was facing many threats; thus the people may have been especially concerned and responsive to any news that God was going to destroy the nation. Yet God was merciful and saved the city when the people repented. This event highlights a clear contrast between the rebellion of the northern kingdom and the repentance of Assyria.

After Shalmaneser IV died, several kings followed who helped Assyria recover its strength. By the mid-700s BC, Assyria had expanded its borders under the leadership of Tiglath-Pileser III (744–727). Through succeeding kings (Sargon II, Sennacherib, Esarhaddon, and Ashurbanipal), Assyria ruled an area extending from Egypt up to Cyprus to the west, through western Anatolia, and over to the Zagros Mountains and the Persian Gulf in the east. By this time, the empire had truly recovered and was once again a major superpower.

The reconstructed Nergal Gate of Nineveh. The wall on the left is original and was built around 700 BC. The original gate was guarded by two stone sculptures of winged bull-men. The Nergal Gate was named after the god of Nineveh named Nergal.

In 722 BC, the Assyrians finally attacked the northern kingdom of Israel. They besieged the capital city of Samaria for three years. Once the city fell, it was burned to the ground, and the surviving population was deported. The region was then resettled with refugees from other Assyrian conquests. These refugees intermarried with the few remaining Jewish survivors, resulting in a group of people with mixed ancestry as well as mixed religious practices (since the refugees also brought with them their pagan religious beliefs and traditions). These people became known as Samaritans, and by the time of Jesus Christ, they were hated by the Jews who were descended from those who eventually returned from captivity and resettled the land.

> **For more on Israel's fall to Assyria, read 2 Kings 17.**

An Assyrian lion-hunting scene. Images like this were common in Assyrian royal art.

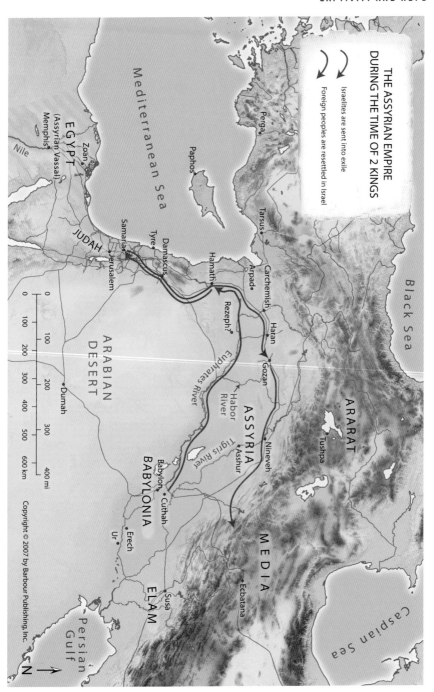

THE ASSYRIAN EMPIRE
DURING THE TIME OF 2 KINGS

Israelites are sent into exile

Foreign peoples are resettled in Israel

Black Sea

Caspian Sea

Mediterranean Sea

Persian Gulf

ARARAT

MEDIA

ASSYRIA

BABYLONIA

ELAM

ARABIAN DESERT

JUDAH

EGYPT
(Assyrian Vassal)

Memphis

Zoan

Nile

Jerusalem

Samaria

Tyre

Damascus

Hamath

Rezeph?

Arpad

Carchemish

Tarsus

Perga

Paphos

Haran

Gozan

Habor River

Euphrates River

Tigris River

Nineveh

Asshur

Babylon

Cuthah

Ur

Erech

Susa

Ecbatana

Tushpa

Dumah

N

0   100   200   300   400   500   600 km
0   100   200   300   400 mi

Copyright © 2007 by Barbour Publishing, Inc.

The author of the book of 2 Kings summarizes the reason for the fall of the northern kingdom at the hands of the Assyrians:

■ *And this occurred because the people of Israel had sinned against the* LORD *their God, who had brought them up out of the land of Egypt from under the hand of Pharaoh king of Egypt, and had feared other gods and walked in the customs of the nations whom the* LORD *drove out before the people of Israel, and in the customs that the kings of Israel had practiced (2 Kings 17:7–8).*

Yet it was not only the northern kingdom that fell; the southern kingdom eventually fell as well, and many people of Judah were carried away into captivity.

THE ASSYRIAN AND BABYLONIAN EMPIRES AND THE SOUTHERN KINGDOM

The history of the southern kingdom of Judah is quite different from that of the northern kingdom. Though Judah had its share of evil kings who turned away from serving God, the nation also had some good kings who sought to be faithful to God. For example, from 740 to 732 BC, Jotham ruled Judah, and he was known as a king who truly obeyed the law of the Lord. As a result of Jotham's obedience, Judah prospered both militarily and economically.

	UNITED KINGDOM	
	Saul	
	David	
	Solomon	
KINGS OF THE NORTHERN KINGDOM		**KINGS OF THE SOUTHERN KINGDOM**
Jeroboam		Rehoboam
Nadab		Abijah
Baasha		Asa
Elah		Jehoshaphat
Zimri		Joram
Omri		Queen Athaliah
Ahab		Joash
Ahaziah		Amaziah
Joram		Uzziah
Ahaziah		Jotham
Jehu		Ahaz
Jehoahaz		Hezekiah
Jehoash		Manasseh
Jeroboam II		Amon
Zechariah		Josiah
Shallum		Jehoahaz
Menahem		Jehoiakim
Pekahiah		Jehoiachin
Pekah		Zedekiah
Hoshea		

THE ASSYRIAN THREAT

The king who followed Jotham was a bad king named Ahaz, who ruled Judah from 732 to 716 BC. The name Ahaz is shortened from Jehoahaz, meaning "possession of Yahweh." It is significant that his name was shortened, because he was so rebellious to the Lord that it was evident he did not belong to Him.

> Ahaz was not like his father at all. As soon as he ascended to the throne, he began to follow Canaanite religious practices, even sacrificing his own children to the false gods of the Canaanites.

Ahaz was not like his father at all. As soon as he ascended to the throne, he began to follow Canaanite religious practices, even sacrificing his own children to the false gods of the Canaanites. Because of the sins of Ahaz, the Lord allowed the Philistines, the Edomites, and the Syrians to invade and conquer the border cities of Judah. It was at this time that Judah lost the port of Elath on the Gulf of Aqaba. (The Gulf is located to the east of the Sinai Peninsula in the photo below. Judah had a port on the northern edge of the Gulf.)

Because of a looming military threat from Aram and Israel, Ahaz made an alliance with the Assyrians, robbing the temple to send money to bribe Tiglath-Pileser for his support. In return, the Assyrians offered to attack Aram and Israel (they had been planning to do so anyway). Isaiah confronted Ahaz about turning to the Assyrians for security and advised him to trust in the Lord instead. He even offered to give Ahaz a sign from the Lord to prove the truth of his words. When Ahaz refused, thereby rejecting help from the Lord, the Lord Himself chose a sign, promising that a child would be born and that before the child had reached a certain age, the kings of Aram and Israel would be overthrown.

It is in the midst of this prophecy to Ahaz that Isaiah told of a coming child whose

name would be Immanuel, literally "God with us" (Isaiah 7:14). The point of this prophecy was twofold: First, the sign meant the certain destruction of Judah. Second, even though Ahaz would not trust in God, God gave a sign to the people of Judah to keep their hope alive that He would make good on His promise that a Messiah was coming. The sign that God gave to Ahaz ultimately pointed to the day when God's King would come and rule, and God Himself would come to this earth to save mankind. This prophecy, given during a time of sin and impending destruction, was a message of future hope. Even at this very dark moment in history, God gave one of the most well-known prophecies in all of scripture:

■ *"Therefore the Lord himself will give you a sign. Behold, the virgin shall conceive and bear a son, and shall call his name Immanuel" (Isaiah 7:14).*

While God's people rebelled against Him, the kingdoms of the world flexed their muscles, and all hope appeared to be lost. But God spoke and told His people that He was coming to save them.

When Tiglath-Pileser III died in 727 BC and the northern kingdom of Israel stopped making payments of the required annual tribute to Assyria, King Ahaz of Judah continued to pay it. As the Assyrians swept down from the north, laying siege to the capital city of Samaria, Ahaz and all Judah watched in fear. For three years, Samaria held out under the siege until famine and disease decimated the population. When the city fell in 721 BC, the surviving population was deported. The northern kingdom of Israel ceased to exist.

WHEN AHAZ DIED, HIS SON HEZEKIAH BECAME THE NEW KING OF JUDAH. HEZEKIAH WAS LIKELY A YOUNG MAN WHEN THE CITY OF SAMARIA FELL; SO HE, ALONG WITH THE REST OF THE PEOPLE OF JUDAH, WOULD HAVE BEEN VERY AWARE OF THE INHUMAN CRUELTIES THE ASSYRIANS INFLICTED ON THE PEOPLE OF THE NORTHERN KINGDOM. AFTER THE FALL OF ISRAEL, THE ASSYRIANS BEGAN TO EYE THE SOUTHERN KINGDOM OF JUDAH AS WELL. IT WAS ONLY A MATTER OF TIME BEFORE THEY WOULD ATTACK. WHAT WOULD THE NEW KING HEZEKIAH DO IN THE FACE OF SUCH MOUNTING PRESSURE? WOULD HE TURN TO GOD OR WOULD HE TRY HUMAN FORMS OF MANIPULATION TO SAVE THE NATION?

Hezekiah was not like his father. He was a good king who did what was right in the eyes of the Lord (2 Kings 18:3). Hezekiah inherited a kingdom that was paying tribute to Assyria to keep them from attacking, but when he took the throne he stopped paying the tribute (2 Kings 18:7). He understood the risk of provoking Assyria, yet he believed that God would be his protector.

Sennacherib, the king of Assyria, mounted an all-out offensive against Judah and brought every weapon at his disposal to attack the kingdom. Yet Hezekiah was told that the city would not be overrun. As the Assyrians besieged Jerusalem, the angel of the Lord went out and struck down 185,000 Assyrian soldiers in one night (2 Kings 19:35). Upon this supernatural defeat, the Assyrians withdrew their attack and Jerusalem was spared destruction.

Shortly after Hezekiah received the word from God that he would be protected (2 Kings 19), he became very sick, to the point of death (2 Kings 20). At first God told him that he would die. But when Hezekiah prayed and asked the Lord to heal him, God heard his prayer and sent the prophet Isaiah to tell Hezekiah that the Lord would heal him. Isaiah ordered that a cake of figs be put on Hezekiah's boil, and the king recovered (2 Kings 20:7).

In 1939 a French excavation of the Phoenician seaport of Ugarit uncovered an ancient book of veterinary medicine. This book contained prescriptions for the

Isaiah visits Hezekiah on his deathbed.
Original date and artist unknown.

treatment of horses. Apparently the book belonged to the captain of the cavalry of the king of Ugarit, and it is dated to around 1500 BC. One of the interesting entries in this book reads as follows: "If a horse has a swollen head or a sore nose, prepare

a salve from figs and raisins, mixed with oatmeal and liquid."*
This was the same mixture that Isaiah prescribed for Hezekiah.
God chose to use the resources of the earth to bring healing to
Hezekiah.

> **For more
> on Judah's
> stand against
> Assyria, read
> 2 Kings 19.**

THE RISE OF BABYLON

After Judah's successful stand against Assyria, and Hezekiah's illness, something happened that brought a prophecy of captivity for the southern kingdom. The king of Babylon, Merodach-baladan, sent envoys to Judah with
letters and a present for Hezekiah in response to his sickness and recovery.
This practice was not unheard of at the time, but it clearly had an agenda
behind it.

In all Babylon, there was no king more aggressive against Assyria than
Merodach-baladan. Beginning in 728 BC, the king of Assyria officially held
the title of king of Babylonia. During that time, Merodach-baladan was a dis-

trict ruler in Chaldea. Around 722, while Assyria
was distracted by some internal political issues,
Merodach-baladan took advantage of the opportunity to declare himself king of Babylon. He then
seceded from the Assyrian Empire and began to
attack it.

From his vantage point, it appeared as if Judah had successfully repelled Assyria during its
siege against Jerusalem, so he used the opportunity created by Hezekiah's sickness to discuss
plans for Judah and Babylon to unite against Assyria. Though scripture does not say this directly,
Hezekiah's willingness to show the Babylonian
envoys all the resources of the nation strongly

The angel of God destroys the Assyrian
camp in 2 Kings 19:35. Originally printed
in 1792 in a Bible published by Thomas
Macklin in London.

suggests that they were comparing resources for the purpose of developing
an attack strategy.

But Hezekiah's actions did not sit well with God, and Isaiah foretold that
a time was coming when the Babylonians would come and take everything
the people of Judah owned. This came true many decades later in 586 BC.
Babylon sacked Jerusalem and took many people from Judah into captivity.

After Hezekiah died, his son Manasseh took the throne. Manasseh was
only twelve years old when he became king of Judah, and he remained king
for the next fifty-five years. Manasseh was known for two things: the longev-
ity of his reign and his extreme wickedness. He rebuilt the altars to Baal that

*Werner Keller, *The Bible as History* (New York: Bantam,
1981), 273.

his father, Hezekiah, had torn down. He also participated in the evil worship practices of Baal that included child sacrifices. Manasseh was an evil man who was responsible for the murder of many faithful people in Judah. The book of 2 Kings describes it well:

■ *And he did what was evil in the sight of the Lord, according to the despicable practices of the nations whom the Lord drove out before the people of Israel. For he rebuilt the high places that Hezekiah his father had destroyed, and he erected altars for Baal and made an Asherah, as Ahab king of Israel had done, and worshiped all the host of heaven and served them. And he built altars in the house of the Lord, of which the Lord had said, "In Jerusalem will I put my name." And he built altars for all the host of heaven in the two courts of the house of the Lord. And he burned his son as an offering and used fortune-telling and omens and dealt with mediums and with necromancers. He did much evil in the sight of the Lord, provoking him to anger. . . . Moreover, Manasseh shed very much innocent blood, till he had filled Jerusalem from one end to another, besides the sin that he made Judah to sin so that they did what was evil in the sight of the Lord (2 Kings 21:2–6, 16).*

A reconstructed altar probably used for animal sacrifice and destroyed during the reign of Hezekiah

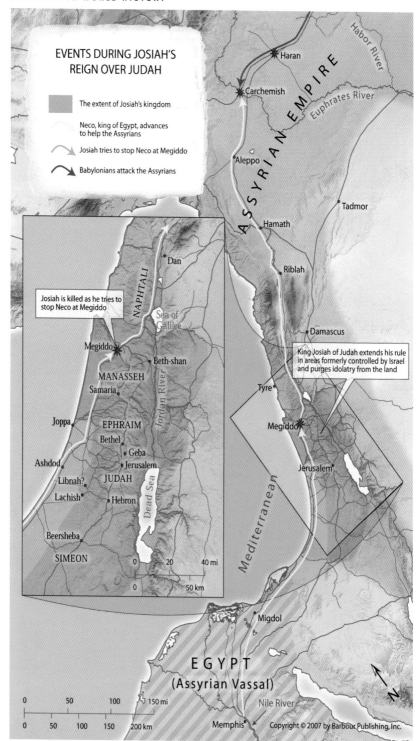

EVENTS DURING JOSIAH'S
REIGN OVER JUDAH

The extent of Josiah's kingdom

Neco, king of Egypt, advances
to help the Assyrians

Josiah tries to stop Neco at Megiddo

Babylonians attack the Assyrians

Josiah is killed as he tries to
stop Neco at Megiddo

King Josiah of Judah extends his rule
in areas formerly controlled by Israel
and purges idolatry from the land

Habor River

Haran

Carchemish

ASSYRIAN EMPIRE

Euphrates River

Aleppo

Tadmor

Hamath

Riblah

Dan

NAPHTALI

Sea of
Galilee

Damascus

Megiddo

Beth-shan

MANASSEH

Samaria

Jordan River

Tyre

Megiddo

Joppa

EPHRAIM

Bethel

Geba

Jerusalem

Ashdod

Jerusalem

Libnah?

JUDAH

Lachish

Hebron

Dead Sea

Mediterranean

Beersheba

SIMEON

0   20   40 mi

0   50 km

Migdol

EGYPT
(Assyrian Vassal)

N

0   50   100   150 mi

0   50   100   150   200 km

Memphis   Copyright © 2007 by Barbour Publishing, Inc.

Nile River

After Manasseh died, his son Amon took the throne. He proved to be just as wicked as his father and continued the evil that Manasseh had begun. Thus, Judah continued its downward spiral into increasingly greater rebellion against God.

While Judah seemed to be in a religious and moral free fall, Babylon continued to gain strength, and Assyria continued to weaken. Eventually the Assyrians began to falter in their ability to hold their empire together, and Babylon captured more and more Assyrian cities. As the Assyrian Empire was on the verge of total collapse, the king of Judah became involved in a way that would change Judah forever.

In Egypt, Pharaoh Neco II took the throne and sought to increase Egypt's influence in world affairs by helping the Assyrians in their fight against the rising Babylonian power. Neco mustered his army and headed north to assist the Assyrians at Carchemish. To get there, however, they needed to pass through territory belonging to Judah and Israel.

The kingdom of Judah, and even much of the territory of the fallen kingdom of Israel, was ruled at that time by Josiah, who had succeeded his father, Amon, as king in 640 BC, and who ruled until 609 BC. Josiah was a good king, who did much to rid Judah of idolatry. He tore down all the altars to Baal that his father and grandfather had constructed. He reasserted his independence from Assyria and sought to establish the strength of Judah once again.

> Neco killed Josiah and continued northward. Josiah's efforts appear to have been somewhat successful, because Neco was unable to reach Carchemish in time.

When Josiah heard about Neco's intentions to assist Assyria, he attempted to halt him at a strategic mountain pass near the town of Megiddo. Neco was not looking to fight against Judah at this point, so he sent a message urging Josiah to let him pass through the region without incident. Josiah refused and attacked Neco's troops at Megiddo. Neco killed Josiah and continued northward. Even so, Josiah's efforts appear to have been somewhat successful, because Neco was unable to reach Carchemish in time to help the Assyrians, who were defeated by the Babylonians.

Left: Map illustrates the route taken by Pharaoh Neco to the battle of Carchemish.
Right: Photo shows a bronze statue of either Pharaoh Neco I or Pharaoh Neco II.

The Fall of Jerusalem. Original artist unknown. Created in France in 1372.

With the fall of Assyria all but complete, the Babylonians were free to claim all of Assyria's former territory, including Israel and Judah. Eventually the kings whom the Babylonians appointed to rule over Judah rebelled, so the Babylonians repeatedly deported Judeans to Babylon and elsewhere. Finally, in 586 BC, King Nebuchadnezzar of Babylon attacked Jerusalem, burning down the city and sending many people into captivity.

The difference between the Babylonian captivity of Judah and the Assyrian captivity of Israel is that the Babylonians brought the key leaders of Judah to Babylon, to use their skills to serve the king, and left the poor and unskilled back in Judah to keep the land. Unlike the Assyrians, they did not merely enslave everyone and make them servants of manual labor. Thus, we see Judeans such as Daniel eventually rise to the position of head of the Magi (see Daniel 4:9).

THE REST OF THE WORLD
605–539 BC

While the Near East was embroiled in war and conquest, the rest of the world was undergoing change as well. Let's look at some strategic countries and the impact of this era on our lives today.

AT THIS TIME, GREECE WAS NOT A UNIFIED COUNTRY. INSTEAD, IT WAS A SERIES OF SEPARATE CITY-STATES THAT WARRED WITH ONE ANOTHER FOR GREATER INFLUENCE. TWO KEY CITY-STATES IN GREECE WERE SPARTA AND ATHENS.

Sparta

The city-state of Sparta, founded around 800 BC, was known as a warrior society. Located in the southern part of the Peloponnese, the large peninsula located southwest of Athens, Sparta controlled most of the region. An intensely militaristic society, they formed their entire city-state around the notion of preparing every generation for war.

When a Spartan boy was born, he was taken by an elder and examined to see if he had any defects that would deem him unfit to live. If he was deemed unfit, he would be left on a hillside exposed to the elements so that he would die. If the boy was chosen to live, he stayed with his family until the age of seven and then was transferred to a military camp, where he would be trained as a soldier. When he turned nineteen, he underwent a rite of passage into adulthood in which he was required to kill a slave without being seen. If the young man was successful, he was considered fit to protect the city, and thus he would be able to join the army. The Spartans were fearless warriors and were the most skilled fighting force in that part of the world.

Athens

Sparta's primary rival was Athens. The Athenians had a system of government that is regarded as the first democracy. The word *democracy* comes from two Greek words: *demos*, which means "people," and *kratos*, which means "power." In short, it is a system of government in which power is extended from the people rather than wielded over the people. We cannot underestimate the importance of the development of rule by democracy. In much of the ancient world, the state derived its power from the king, who held a position of such power that, in some cases, he was even regarded as divine. Athens took the power of government away from a single leader and put it into the hands of the people. How did this work?

Athenian democracy was different from the form of democracy typically practiced today. The biggest difference is that the Athenian version was extraordinarily direct rather than being representative, as it is in the United States. For the most part, Athenians did not vote for politicians to represent them. Every law or policy was voted on directly by the people. Because of this, government officials held a limited role.

Though public officials did run the government, they did not have the scope of power that officials have in the United States today. The Athenians took radical measures to limit the power of their government—such as choosing officials by lot. This allowed for absolutely anyone to hold a position in the government, rather than enabling an elite class to amass so much influence or power that they were difficult to remove from office.

During this same era, a Greek mathematician named Pythagoras derived a theorem to determine the unknown length of one side of a right triangle when the lengths of the other two sides are known. Every high school student who has taken geometry has learned the Pythagorean theorem.

SPARTA

Above: Marble statue of a soldier from Sparta
Right: Statue of Leonidas in Thermopylae, Greece
Below: Landscape of modern Sparta

Most of the information we have about Pythagoras was recorded centuries after he lived; thus very few reliable facts are known about him. Nevertheless, it is likely he was born in 570 BC on the Greek island of Samos, just off the western coast of Turkey; and it is possible he traveled extensively in his youth. Around 530 BC, he moved to Croton, a Greek colony in southern Italy, where he set up a religious sect based upon his spiritual interest in mathematics.

Pythagoras assigned mystical significance to numbers and believed that the spiritual world could be understood through the order and logic of mathematics. For this reason, music was also very important to Pythagoras. He saw that musical pitches could be broken down and understood in light of

ATHENS

Above: The ancient theater of Athens, Greece.
Below: Temple of Athena, Athens

Section of a woodcut showing Pythagoras with bells in Pythagorean tuning. From *Theorica musicae* by Franchino Gaffurio, late fifteenth century.

mathematical ratios. The basic musical scale finds its roots in Pythagorean logic.

Followers of Pythagoras applied his mathematical ideas to medicine, astronomy, and natural science. His works and ideas shaped the philosophy of many who came after him, and the impact of his mathematical understanding of the world led to some very powerful advancements. His ideas led to a form of reasoning that allowed people to deconstruct ideas, music, nature, medicine, and a host of other things so that we can quantify their parts and understand how they work.

THE DEVELOPMENT OF BUDDHISM

The world is much bigger, of course, than simply Europe and the Near East. In Nepal, for example, in the Far East, a philosophical awakening was under way that would have a lasting effect on millions of people down through the ages.

While Greece was developing politically, militarily, and philosophically, a clan called the Shakyas ruled over a small region in the Himalayan Mountains in what is now southern Nepal. The head of this clan, and the king of the region, was named Suddhodana Gautama, and his wife was named Mahamaya. When Mahamaya was expecting her firstborn child, she had a strange dream in which a baby elephant blessed her with its trunk. This was understood to be a very important sign. Mahamaya eventually gave birth to a son, and they named him Siddhartha.

After Siddhartha was born, King Suddhodana consulted Asita, a well-known soothsayer, concerning the future of his son. Asita proclaimed that Siddhartha would be one of two things: either he would become a great king, and maybe even an emperor, or he would become a great sage and spiritual leader. The king, eager that his son should become a king, determined to shield Siddhartha from anything that might lead him to pursue religion.

Right: The Himalayan Mountains were the birthplace of Buddhism.

Thus, the boy was not allowed to leave the palace for fear he might see something that would pierce his heart and drive him to a religious life. Siddhartha was not permitted to see the elderly, the sick, the dead, or any persons who had dedicated themselves to spiritual practices. His father wanted him to witness only beauty and health so that he would love the palace and desire to rule the kingdom one day.

Siddhartha grew to be a strong and skillful young man. As a prince of the warrior caste, he trained and excelled in the art of war. When it came time for him to marry, he won the hand of a beautiful princess, Yashodhara, from a neighboring kingdom, by besting all competitors at a variety of sports. They married when both were sixteen years old.

However, as Siddhartha continued living in luxury, he grew increasingly curious about the world outside the palace walls. He finally demanded to see the people and the land that he was to rule one day. The king allowed this to happen but still carefully arranged for Siddhartha not to see the kind of suffering that his father feared would lead him to a religious life. He did this

Above: A painting in a Laotian temple (original artist unknown). It portrays the people Siddhartha saw as he left the temple. Right: A Buddhist temple in Myanmar.

by removing all the sick and elderly from around the palace so that his son would see only health and beauty.

As Siddhartha was led through Kapilavatthu, the capital, he chanced to see a couple of old men who had accidentally wandered near. Amazed and confused, he chased after them to find out what they were. Next, he came across some people who were severely ill. Finally, he came across a funeral ceremony by the side of a river, and for the first time in his life, he saw death. He asked his friend and squire, Chandaka, the meaning of all these things, and Chandaka informed him of the simple truth that everyone grows old, becomes sick, and eventually dies. Siddhartha also saw a monk who had renounced all the pleasures of the flesh. The peaceful look on the monk's face burned an image in Siddhartha's mind that never left him.

> At the age of twenty-nine, Siddhartha came to realize that he could not be happy living as he had been. He had discovered suffering, and now he wanted more than anything to discover how one might overcome suffering.

At the age of twenty-nine, Siddhartha came to realize that he could not

be happy living as he had been. He had discovered suffering, and now he wanted more than anything to discover how one might overcome suffering. After kissing his sleeping wife and newborn son, Rahula, good-bye, he slipped out of the palace with his faithful squire. He gave away his rich clothing, cut his long hair, and gave his favorite horse, Kanthaka, to Chandaka, telling him to return to the palace. Siddhartha then started on a long journey, on which he finally found nirvana, a state of inner peace and perfect harmony. When Siddhartha attained what he considered to be nirvana, he was then called the Buddha. The Buddhist religion, which is still practiced by millions today, is centered on the teachings of peace and enrichment that Siddhartha discovered on his journey.

Let's now return to the Near East and pick up the story of the people of Judah in Babylonian captivity.

JUDAH IN CAPTIVITY

As we noted earlier, the Babylonians were different from the Assyrians and the Egyptians in the way they treated captives from conquered lands. The Babylonians selected young men of skill and utilized them as government officials, rather than making them slaves and consigning them to simple, unskilled labor. When the Babylonians took the people of Judah captive, the brightest young men of the nation were brought to the capital and trained for positions of leadership.

One of these young men was Daniel, a faithful Jew whom God would use in very powerful ways. The event that elevated Daniel to a critical position of leadership involved his interpretation of a dream.

Daniel among the Exiles.
Engraving by Gustave Doré (1832–1883).

At this pivotal moment in world history, God told the pagan king of Babylon how the future of the world would play out. Let's look more closely at this important event, which is recorded in the book of Daniel.

NEBUCHADNEZZAR'S DREAM

Daniel chapter 2 records how King Nebuchadnezzar of Babylon had a dream that disturbed him so much that he called for his magicians and wise men to interpret it. The king set the condition that the wise men must also be able to tell him the dream, because he wanted to make sure that he received the proper interpretation. When none of the magicians and wise men were able to tell the king his dream, Nebuchadnezzar ordered them all to be killed. When Daniel heard this, he prayed to God, and God revealed to him both the dream and the interpretation of the dream:

> For more on the king's dream, read Daniel 2.

■ *"You saw, O king, and behold, a great image. This image, mighty and of exceeding brightness, stood before you, and its appearance was frightening. The head of this image was of fine gold, its chest and arms of silver, its middle and thighs of bronze, its legs of iron, its feet partly of iron and partly of clay. As you looked, a stone was cut out by no human hand, and it struck the image on its feet*

Excavations of the ancient city of Babylon

of iron and clay, and broke them in pieces. Then the iron, the clay, the bronze, the silver, and the gold, all together were broken in pieces, and became like the chaff of the summer threshing floors; and the wind carried them away, so that not a trace of them could be found" (Daniel 2:31–35).

KING NEBUCHADNEZZAR WAS ARGUABLY THE MIGHTIEST KING IN THE WORLD AT THAT TIME. HE HAD CONQUERED EVERYONE AND EVERYTHING IN HIS PATH. BUT AT THE TIME OF THIS DREAM, HE WAS SIDELINED. HE WAS NOT THE CENTER OF HIS DREAM; THE STATUE WAS. HE WAS NOT A CONQUEROR; HE WAS JUST AN OBSERVER.

> He saw the kingdom of God smash the kingdoms of this world, and there was nothing he could do about it. Perhaps that is one of the things that scared him so much in the dream.

Nebuchadnezzar might have thought that he was the great conqueror and that nothing could stop him from building his kingdom, but in this divine dream he was nothing; he was simply watching it all happen. He saw the kingdom of God smash the kingdoms of this world, and there was nothing he could do about it. Perhaps that is one of the things that scared him so much in the dream. It must have scared him to come across something or someone more powerful than he.

If you've ever walked past a tall skyscraper like Chicago's Sears Tower (now called the Willis Tower), you know you can walk right up next to the building and look straight up. It can be frightening to feel so insignificant next to a towering structure. This may be a glimpse of how Nebuchadnezzar felt seeing the enormous statue in his dream. As he watched the sovereign God of the universe control the events of mankind, perhaps it challenged his ego and revealed to him that he was really nothing.

■ *"But the stone that struck the image became a great mountain and filled the whole earth" (Daniel 2:35).*

Through this dream, God allowed Nebuchadnezzar to come face-to-face with the future, which was under God's control and not Nebuchadnezzar's. Nebuchadnezzar believed that his destiny was immortality and eternal kingship over Babylon, yet God was saying that his future would not be as bright as he thought.

AFTER DANIEL FINISHED RECOUNTING THE DREAM, HE EXPLAINED ITS MEANING TO THE KING, OFFERING NEBUCHADNEZZAR THE FIRST OF MANY LESSONS ABOUT THE SOVEREIGNTY OF GOD. THROUGH THIS DREAM, GOD REVEALED THAT THE ESSENTIAL ISSUE IN LIFE IS THE KINGDOM OF GOD. THE KINGDOM OF THE WORLD IS GOING TO COME CRASHING DOWN. EVEN THOUGH IT APPEARS AS IF IT IS GOING TO FLOURISH FOREVER, IT WILL NOT. DANIEL'S INTERPRETATION FOCUSED ON FOUR WORLD EMPIRES, THE FIRST OF WHICH WAS NEBUCHAD-NEZZAR'S. EACH SECTION OF THE STATUE REPRESENTED A DIFFERENT NATION.

The First Kingdom

■ *"This was the dream. Now we will tell the king its interpretation. You, O king, the king of kings, to whom the God of heaven has given the kingdom, the power, and the might, and the glory, and into whose hand he has given, wherever they dwell, the children of man, the beasts of the field, and the birds of the heavens, making you rule over them all—you are the head of gold" (Daniel 2:36–38).*

Daniel told the king that he was the head of this statue. Notice the way in which Daniel began his interpretation. He called Nebuchadnezzar the "king of kings." Some might be a little surprised at this. Here, this title does not refer to the Messiah, Jesus, who is also called the King of kings or, literally, the King to whom all other kings are subject. Nebuchadnezzar is called the king of kings because he is the one who is the representative of all the kingdoms of the world. Furthermore, from its first mention in Genesis 10:8–12, Babylon has always stood for that which is opposed to God. Nebuchadnezzar is the king over all the other kings in his empire, which means all the kings who are opposed to God.

Augustine, the great church scholar and theologian, wrote a monumental work during the fall of the Roman Empire called *The City of God*, in which he talked about this very concept, saying that there are really only two kingdoms: the kingdom of man, which serves itself, and the kingdom of God, which serves the Lord. Nebuchadnezzar was the head of gold on the statue, because his kingdom was the most glorious of all of the kingdoms of the world. Still to date, there has not been a kingdom that has matched the glory and splendor of the great Babylon. The gardens of Babylon are considered one of the wonders of the ancient world. Therefore, Nebuchadnezzar was the head of the statue as the greatest picture of what man can accomplish on this earth.

Augustine

The Second Kingdom

■ *"Another kingdom inferior to you shall arise after you" (Daniel 2:39).*

Notice the next kingdom and the way it is described. This nation, which would conquer Babylon, would be "inferior" to Babylon. This is a very strange way to describe a kingdom. The reason for this description is that even though the next kingdom would be stronger, it would not be as glorious. That is why it is represented in the statue as silver, which is stronger than gold but less glorious. This kingdom was the kingdom of the Medes and the Persians.

This part of the interpretation revealed to King Nebuchadnezzar that his days were numbered and that another kingdom would soon come that would conquer Babylon. Yet even this new kingdom would not last forever, for a third kingdom would come to conquer the second.

The Third Kingdom

■ *"And yet a third kingdom of bronze, which shall rule over all the earth"* (Daniel 2:39).

Just as bronze is stronger than silver and even stronger than gold, it is also less glorious than both. Thus, this bronze portion of the statue represented the Greek kingdom of Alexander the Great, which was stronger than the previous two kingdoms, but less glorious.

Alexander the Great with Aristotle. Original artist and date unknown.

The Fourth Kingdom

■ *"And there shall be a fourth kingdom, strong as iron, because iron breaks to pieces and shatters all things. And like iron that crushes, it shall break and crush all these"* (Daniel 2:40).

After the Greek Empire, the mighty Roman Empire would emerge and conquer everything. This kingdom would be the strongest of all kingdoms; but again, it would be the least of all in terms of glory. It would not even come close to matching the majesty of the Babylonian Empire. Yet when the Romans emerged, they established a very strong kingdom that lasted for quite some time. Notice one important aspect of this kingdom:

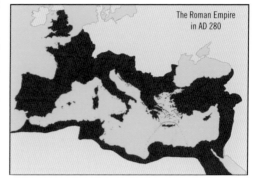

The Roman Empire in AD 280

■ *"And as you saw the feet and toes, partly of potter's clay and partly of iron, it shall be a divided kingdom, but some of the firmness of iron shall be in it, just as you saw iron mixed with the soft clay. And as the toes of the feet were partly iron and partly clay, so the kingdom shall be partly strong and partly brittle. As you saw the iron mixed with soft clay, so they will mix with one another in marriage, but they will not hold together, just as iron does not mix with clay"* (Daniel 2:41–43).

DANIEL TOLD NEBUCHADNEZZAR THAT THIS FOURTH NATION WOULD HAVE FEET OF BOTH IRON AND CLAY, WHICH DO NOT BOND TOGETHER. THOUGH THE ROMAN EMPIRE WAS STRONG, IT NEVER HAD TRUE UNITY. IT WAS PLAGUED BY CIVIL WARS, SOCIAL UNREST, AND MORAL RELATIVISM. THEREFORE, IN THE STRENGTH OF ROME THERE WAS ALSO WEAKNESS. IT COULD NOT REMAIN STRONG AT ALL POINTS, FOR THE PEOPLE WERE CONSTANTLY RISING UP AGAINST IT OR SIDING WITH ITS ENEMIES. YET IN THE AREAS WHERE ROME WAS STRONG, IT WAS VERY STRONG.

The Eternal Kingdom

This prophecy, however, was not merely God's way of showing King Nebuchadnezzar how the world would take shape over the next several hundred

Nebuchadnezzar's statue

years. The rest of the prophecy deals with God's greater purpose:

> ■ *"And in the days of those kings the God of heaven will set up a kingdom that shall never be destroyed, nor shall the kingdom be left to another people. It shall break in pieces all these kingdoms and bring them to an end, and it shall stand forever, just as you saw that a stone was cut from a mountain by no human hand, and that it broke in pieces the iron, the bronze, the clay, the silver, and the gold. A great God has made known to the king what shall be after this. The dream is certain, and its interpretation sure"* (Daniel 2:44–45).

One thing to keep in mind is that even though four kingdoms are mentioned in the vision, together they comprise one statue. That is because these four nations represent a one-world system. These four nations are the governing nations that rule and reign from Nebuchadnezzar's time until the coming of the Messiah. And because the Messiah comes, the system of the world eventually collapses.

THE POINT OF THE PROPHECY IS THAT MAN IS OPPOSED TO GOD, BUT GOD WILL DESTROY MAN'S SYSTEM; IT WILL NOT STAND FOREVER. THE KINGDOM OF MAN IN ALL ITS GLORY AND STRENGTH WILL NOT BE ABLE TO STAND BEFORE THE KINGDOM OF GOD. THIS DREAM SPEAKS OF A DESTRUCTION OF THE NATIONS BY A ROCK THAT IS CUT WITHOUT HANDS, AND IT SMASHES THE ROMAN EMPIRE, CAUSING THE ENTIRE STATUE TO COME CRASHING DOWN. THIS ROCK IS THE KINGDOM OF GOD; AND AS WE WILL SEE IN DANIEL CHAPTER 7, THIS KINGDOM IS RULED BY THE ANCIENT OF DAYS, WHO IS JESUS HIMSELF. THIS KINGDOM WILL DESTROY THE KINGDOM OF THE WORLD.

Why did God go to such effort to reveal that His kingdom would smash the kingdoms of man? To grasp this, we must understand the point of the book of Daniel. This book was written to show the Jews that God is sovereign and that nothing is outside of His control. More specifically, even Israel's domination by the Babylonians was part of God's plan. Though nations rise, they do so because God allows them, and they fall because God knocks them down. The rock that destroys the kingdom is cut from a mountain, which is the immovable, eternal kingdom of God.

> One thing to keep in mind is that even though four kingdoms are mentioned in the vision, together they comprise one statue. That is because these four nations represent a one-world system.

Ultimately, God showed both Nebuchadnezzar and Israel (through Daniel's words) that Babylon was just a tool in the hand of God and that another nation would come and destroy it. This new nation would in turn be destroyed and so on, until the kingdom of God came to earth and destroyed the kingdoms of the world.

Understanding this crucial point leads to a change in the way we view the world system today. Practically speaking, the kingdom of God has broken the power of the world, and one day we will see God's kingdom come to completion when Jesus replaces the governments of the world with His perfect government (Revelation 11:15). This is where history is headed, and this is the hope we have in this world as we deal with the rise and fall of nations around us.

THE RETURN
539–500 BC

As Daniel's interpretation had revealed, the kingdom of Babylon would not last forever. After Nebuchadnezzar died, the kingdom began to fall apart. In the years after his death, several kings ruled the empire for short periods of time. Finally, after seven years of very brief reigns, Belshazzar (whom Daniel calls the son of Nebuchadnezzar) came to the throne and ruled for about seventeen years.

In the seventeenth year of Belshazzar's reign, when the Medes and the Persians threatened to attack, the king carelessly ignored the threat and

The story of Daniel in the lions' den occurs in chapter 6 of Daniel. This mosaic may have been created in the fifth century.

instead feasted in Babylon. At one point during the feast, Belshazzar decided to praise his own gods and mock the God of Israel by bringing out the sacred vessels from the temple in Jerusalem (which Nebuchadnezzar had taken when he conquered Judah and destroyed the temple) and drinking from them. Such blasphemy brought immediate and horrible consequences for Belshazzar when a hand appeared in the air and wrote something on the wall.

Seeing this apparition, the king began to tremble with fear, and he cried aloud for his religious leaders to be brought in to read and interpret the writing on the wall. The wise men of Babylon came, but none were able to interpret the handwriting. Finally, the queen came into the banquet house and told Belshazzar that there was a man in the kingdom, Daniel, who could read the writing.

Relief of the Medes and Persians

When Daniel was brought in, the king told him that if he read the words on the wall, he would be rewarded with great wealth. However, Daniel refused the rewards. He reminded Belshazzar of Nebuchadnezzar's painful lessons from God. Then he said that Belshazzar had become just as proud as Nebuchadnezzar and would face certain destruction. At last, Daniel read the words on the wall:

■ *"MENE, MENE, TEKEL, and PARSIN. This is the interpretation of the matter: MENE, God has numbered the days of your kingdom and brought it to an end; TEKEL, you have been weighed in the balances and found wanting; PERES, your kingdom is divided and given to the Medes and Persians"* (Daniel 5:25–28).

The king immediately rewarded Daniel as he had promised. Nevertheless, that very night the armies of Media and Persia conquered the city of Babylon, Belshazzar was slain, and the Babylonian kingdom fell. In its place rose the kingdom represented by silver in Nebuchadnezzar's vision—that of the Medes and the Persians. It was during this dynasty, under the reign of

Cyrus, that the Jews were allowed to return home to Israel in order to help repair the ruined temple.

Cyrus the Great was truly a unique king. After conquering Babylon, he made some changes to the empire that were unheard of in the ancient world. The changes began with the way he viewed his role as king. He did not see

Belshazzar of Babylon portrayed by Rembrandt (1606–1669)

himself as a conqueror, but more as a liberator. He loved the idea of not only taking over the Babylonian Empire, but also freeing those whom the Babylonians had displaced and returning to them some of the freedoms and liberties they had lost.

His view of religious tolerance was unprecedented. Cyrus believed that every god that had been captured by Nebuchadnezzar should be returned to its home and worshipped in its own temple. This led to a declaration that the Jews who had been exiled to Babylon could go back to their homeland and rebuild the temple of the Lord in Jerusalem.

The book of Ezra recounts the reasons that Cyrus made this decree:

■ *In the first year of Cyrus king of Persia, that the word of the LORD by the mouth of Jeremiah might be fulfilled, the LORD stirred up the spirit of Cyrus king of Persia, so that he made a proclamation throughout all his kingdom and also put it in writing: "Thus says Cyrus king of Persia: The LORD, the God of heaven, has given me all the kingdoms of the earth, and he has charged me to build him a house at Jerusalem, which is in Judah. Whoever is among you of all his people, may his God be with him, and let him go up to Jerusalem, which is*

in Judah, and rebuild the house of the LORD, *the God of Israel—he is the God who is in Jerusalem. And let each survivor, in whatever place he sojourns, be assisted by the men of his place with silver and gold, with goods and with beasts, besides freewill offerings for the house of God that is in Jerusalem"* (Ezra 1:1–4).

Cyrus's decision to offer religious tolerance was not just something he dreamed up out of the blue; rather, it was put in his heart by God. Why did God give this to him? Scripture tells us that God had not planned to keep the Israelites in captivity indefinitely. Instead, He used Cyrus to end the captivity and allow the Israelites to return to their land to live, work, and worship as He had planned. Once again, as we take notice of the clear intersection of sacred and secular history, we see that God is the God of all history.

ONE OF THE GREAT ARCHAEOLOGICAL DISCOVERIES MADE FROM THIS TIME PERIOD IS WHAT IS KNOWN AS THE CYRUS CYLINDER. DISCOVERED IN 1879 AMONG THE RUINS OF BABYLON, THIS CYLINDER PROVIDES INSIGHT INTO CYRUS'S REIGN AND THE UNIQUE WAY HE RULED HIS EMPIRE. IT INCLUDES A DETAILED ACCOUNT (IN A LANGUAGE KNOWN AS AKKADIAN CUNEIFORM) OF CYRUS'S CONQUEST OF BABYLON IN 539 BC AND HIS SUBSEQUENT TREATMENT OF THOSE HE HAD CONQUERED. HE WANTED TO BE KNOWN AS A HUMANITARIAN AND AS ONE WHO WOULD TREAT HIS SUBJECTS HUMANELY. MANY HAVE HAILED THIS CYLINDER AS THE WORLD'S FIRST DECLARATION OF HUMAN RIGHTS.

Right: Plaque on display at the House of Public Relations International Cottages at Balboa Park, San Diego, CA (USA)

THE CYRUS CYLINDER

The cylinder is damaged, but what remains outlines the unethical and criminal offenses of the last Babylonian king, Nabonidus. It then records how the Babylonian god Marduk looked for a replacement for Nabonidus and

منشور حقوق بشر کورش بزرگ

First Declaration of Human Rights by Cyrus the Great
Inscribed in cuneiform on a clay cylinder discovered in 1879,
now on display in the British Museum.

Cyrus the Great (585-529 BC), the Iranian emperor, defined the First Declaration of Human Rights on this cylinder. Cyrus is admired more as a liberator than a conqueror of his vast empire because of his respect for human rights and the humane treatment of those he ruled. He is "anointed" in the Bible (Is. 45:4) as a liberator of God's people (Is. 45:15) and the chosen one (Is. 48:14-15). Professor Richard Frye of Harvard University said; *"Surely the concept of One World, the fusion of Peoples and Cultures into oneness was one of his important legacies"*. The following from this ancient cylinder are a rendition of the spirit of his message in modern English:

1. I declare that I will respect the tradition, customs and religion of the nations of my empire and never let any of my governors to look down or insult the inhabitants of my nations.

2. I hereby abolish slavery; my governors are ordered to prohibit exchanging men and women as slaves within their ruling domains. Such a tradition should be exterminated the world over.

3. If anyone oppresses others, should it happen, I will take his/her right back and penalize the oppressors.

4. Today I declare Freedom of Religion. All are free to choose any religion, live in all regions and take up any job provided that they never violate other's rights.

These proclamations ring true today in our times as they did in 538 BC.

House Of Iran

Cyrus the Great

chose Cyrus. Later, it explains how Cyrus established peace and abolished forced labor. It also details his religious tolerance and his restoration of the local gods to their original shrines in their homelands. The essential message of the cylinder is that Cyrus was a liberator and not a dictator.

Part of the text inscribed on the cylinder has become known today as the Cyrus Charter of Human Rights, and a translation of it is on display at the United Nations. A portion of the charter reads as follows:

I am Cyrus. King of the world. When I entered Babylon. . .I did not allow anyone to terrorize the land. . . . I kept in view the needs of people and all its sanctuaries to promote their well-being. . . . I put an end to their misfortune. The Great God has delivered all the lands into my hand; the lands that I have made to dwell in a peaceful habitation. . . . When my soldiers in great numbers peacefully entered Babylon. . .I did not allow anyone to terrorize the people. . . . I kept in view the needs of people and all its sanctuaries to promote their well-being. . . Freed all the slaves. . . I put an end to their misfortune and slavery. The Great God has delivered all the lands into my hand; the lands that I have made to dwell in a peaceful habitation.

REFLECTIONS

In the midst of such power shifts and changes, God speaks, and His important words give us hope. There is nothing more discouraging than to witness wars, pain, misery, suffering, and death. Yet, as we have seen, even when the people of God were in their darkest moments, God spoke to them words of hope.

As we reflect on the events described in this chapter, we are reminded of several other truths as well. Through the prophet Hosea we see that no matter what sins we have committed, God has laid out a path of repentance for us. Through Isaiah we see the hope that God Himself will come to earth to help His people. Through Daniel we see that God is always in control of this world and that no king, no matter how evil, can wrest that power away from Him. Through Cyrus we see that God can

> Even when the people of God were in their darkest moments, God spoke to them words of hope.

use even a pagan king to bring about great good for His people.

In light of what God has said at this point in history, we see that, in Jesus, God has broken the ultimate power of evil and has provided a way for mankind to be made spiritually free from bondage to sin. One day, God will even free us from the very presence of evil in the world. We must not succumb to the fear that evil will be victorious over Christ. Instead, we must always remember that though evil may seem to prosper for a time, ultimately it will be destroyed. No kingdom has ever done away with the church, nor has any sin ever done in the church. God's kingdom will last forever.

TIME LINE
750 BC – 500 BC

BIBLE EVENT · WORLD EVENT

NORTHERN KINGDOM
Dates when they begin reign

SOUTHERN KINGDOM
Dates when they begin reign

750

742—Pekahiah
740—Pekah

732—Hoshea
722—Fall of Israel

PROPHETS
738—Micah begins ministry

732—Ahaz

716—Hezekiah

700

697—Manasseh

658—Nahum begins ministry
650—Jeremiah begins ministry

643—Amon
640—Zephaniah begins ministry   640—Josiah

650

620—Birth of Daniel
620—Ezekiel begins ministry

608—Habakkuk begins
       ministry

590—Obadiah begins ministry

609—Jehoahaz
609—Jehoiakim

600

598—Jehoiachin
597—Zedekiah
586—Fall of Judah

550

522—Zechariah begins ministry
520—Haggai begins ministry

500

750—Greece settles Sicily
744—Tiglath-Pileser III reigns in Assyria

726—Shalmaneser V reigns in Assyria
722—Sargon II reigns in Assyria and conquers the
       northern kingdom

704—Sennacherib reigns in Assyria

660—Japanese culture begins to emerge

612—Nineveh falls to the Babylonians
609—Pharaoh Neco battles in Carchemesh but is
       hindered en route by Josiah
605—Nebuchadnezzar II reigns in Babylon
586—Nebuchadnezzar attacks Judah
570—Confucius teaches in China

539—Cyrus the Great begins reign in Persia
539—Persia conquers Babylon; Darius the Mede
       reigns in Babylon
538—Cyrus allows the Jews to return to Israel
536—The Jews begin rebuilding the temple
521—Darius reigns in Persia
509—Establishment of the Roman Republic

All dates are approximate.

CHAPTER 6

WAR, RESTORATION, AND REFLECTION

SETTING THE STAGE
500–400 BC

Every so often, a period of history arises in which so many political revolutions or technological advancements occur that the period calls for very careful and detailed study if we are to understand its lasting impact on humanity. In this chapter, we will examine just such a time—a single century. During the brief historical period between 500 and 400 BC, many key events occurred that forever altered the history of the world, and the history of Israel in particular. Some of the more significant events of this period include the return of the Jews to the land of Israel (with the subsequent attempt to rebuild the temple), the battle at

Socrates

Thermopylae, the teachings of Socrates and Confucius, and the penning of some very rich books of the Bible (Ezra, Nehemiah, and Esther).

Much like the modern twentieth century, the fourth century BC was marked by continual warfare. In studying it, we will be exposed to much violence and bloodshed. Yet this century was also marked by restoration. The Jewish people were allowed to return to their land and worship Yahweh in their own (rebuilt) temple. This century also experienced great advancement in ideas of humanitarian rights and witnessed (unsuccessful) attempts to eliminate war and aggression. All the while, God continued to fulfill His promises to Israel and to set the stage for the coming of the Messiah.

WAR

Benjamin Franklin once quipped that only two things in life are certain: death and taxes. It could be argued that a third item should be added to his list: war. The previous chapter discussed Nebuchadnezzar's dream, through which God revealed the progression of empires that would come after Babylon. One thing all these kingdoms had in common was their ascension through war and bloodshed. As we now turn our attention to the

Top left: Socrates. Right: Confucius.

Persians, we will see that they, too, continued to experience war even after they conquered Babylon.

The Persian Empire was the largest empire in the ancient world. It covered a region even larger than the mighty Roman Empire, which would eventually come after it.

This art appears on an ancient Greek vase. Based on the inscription found on the vase, Achilles is applying aid to Patroclus, who is suffering from an arrow wound. Vase is dated ca. 500 BC.

THE PERSIAN EMPIRE

One of the unique features of the Persian Empire was that their leaders did not compel the people they conquered to worship Persian gods. Instead, they allowed freedom of religion. Typically in times of conquest, the victorious nation would carry off the idols of the vanquished people and place them in a temple that served as a pantheon of conquered gods. The belief was that as they collected gods, they would be collecting power.

When the Babylonians conquered Israel, they took the gold and the silver from the temple in Jerusalem and brought it to their temple, thereby adding Yahweh to their collection of gods. When the Persians defeated the Babylonians, however, all the gods that the Babylonians had captured were returned to their temples, and the people the Babylonians had displaced were allowed to return home. It was under this policy

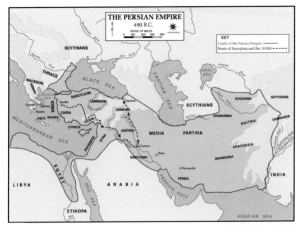

The extent of the Persian Empire

that the Jews were allowed to return to Jerusalem to rebuild their temple. This was a major political freedom that Israel experienced under Persian rule.

Before we look at the wars that occupied much of Persian history, let's examine a few of the kings who ruled over the empire. Rather than list all the kings of Persia, we will look at a few select kings who played an especially significant role in world history. The following chart gives the typical English name used to refer to each king, along with the king's biblical name and the biblical texts in which these kings appear.

ENGLISH NAME	DATE (BC)	BIBLE NAME	BIBLE BACKGROUND
CYRUS	539–530	CYRUS	EZRA 1–3; ISAIAH 45; DANIEL
CAMBYSES	530–521	AHASUERUS	EZRA 4–6
PSEUDO SMERDIS	521	ARTAXERXES	EZRA 4:7–23
DARIUS THE GREAT	521–486	DARIUS	EZRA 5–6
XERXES	486–465	AHASUERUS	ESTHER 1–10
ARTAXERXES I	464–423	ARTAXERXES	EZRA 7–10; NEHEMIAH 1–13

The book of Ezra mentions all the kings listed in the box on the previous page. With several names in common, it is important to understand which king is mentioned in each chapter. For our purposes here, we are going to skip the first three kings on the list and focus on Darius the Great.

Under Darius's leadership, the Persian Empire expanded to its largest size. Shortly before the empire reached its zenith, however, a small rebellion occurred in the region of Ionia in western Asia Minor. During that rebellion,

the city-states of Athens and Eretria sent soldiers to help fight against Persia.

The rebellion in Ionia was squelched, but Darius never forgot the support that the Greeks had given to those who rebelled. His desire for revenge led him to send soldiers to attack the city-states of Athens and Eretria, thus sparking a series of conflicts now known as the Greco-Persian Wars.

The first Persian invasion of Greece began in 492 BC, and it ended with the decisive Athenian victory at the Battle of Marathon in 490 BC. The Battle

This inscription was found in eastern Turkey and is a message from King Xerxes. An excerpt of the inscription reads: "Ahuramazda is the great god, the greatest god who created the sky and created the land and created humans. Who gave prosperity to the humans. Who made Xerxes King of many kings. He is the only ruler of the totality of all lands. I am Xerxes, the great king, the king of kings, the king of the lands, king of all the languages, king of the great and large land, the son of King Darius the Achaemenian."

> The Greeks developed a strategy by which they divided the Persian army and repelled them, sending them into retreat.

of Marathon is the inspiration for one of the most prestigious competitions in the Olympics: the marathon run. When the Persians attacked the Athenians at Marathon, they outnumbered them by as much as two to one. The Greeks, however, developed a strategy by which they divided the Persian army and repelled them, sending them into retreat. According to legend, a Greek soldier named Pheidippides ran from Marathon to Athens to declare that the Greeks had won. It is said that he ran the entire distance without stopping (about twenty-six miles, thus the length of a modern marathon run), and when he arrived and delivered his message, he died on the spot.

After the loss, the Persians retreated and sought to regroup for another attack, but then Darius died and the attack never took place. His son Xerxes then became king and soon took up the cause against the Greeks.

When Xerxes gathered a large fighting force to advance against Greece, the Greeks quickly realized that their infantry would be vastly outnumbered by the Persians. They devised a plan to delay the Persians long enough to allow the Greek navy to attack them. The Greeks sought to force the Persians to fight them in a narrow coastal pass called Thermopylae, which would take away the advantage of the larger force by limiting the number of men who

This relief of King Xerxes was discovered in Persepolis (in modern-day Iran).

could engage in battle at any one time. Also, the Persians would not be able to surround and overwhelm the Greeks by sheer numbers alone, and their vast army would become bottlenecked in the tight pass, unable to move forward rapidly to engage in battle. The strategy was a long shot, but it was the only thing that seemed to hold out any hope of success for the Greeks.

The fearsome Spartans of southern Greece, along with a handful of other Greek troops, were selected to guard the pass. When the Persians attacked, the Spartans pulled back, drawing the Persian troops deeper into the narrow pass and committing them to fight the Greeks within a confined area. The Persians sustained enormous casualties in their clashes with the highly disciplined Spartans, who held their positions in the face of grave danger. Wave upon wave of Persian soldiers moved forward only to meet their death like the others who had gone before them. This went on for two days.

It was only after a local peasant betrayed his countrymen by telling Xerxes about a path that went around the Greek position that the Persians were able to break the bottleneck. They then sent troops to outflank the Greek forces and attack them from behind. Now fighting on two fronts, the Spartans made a final stand before the Persians killed them off and advanced through the pass. Despite the tragic outcome, the battle at Thermopylae has always been hailed as a triumph for the Greeks because it delayed the Persian army long enough for the rest of the Greeks to flee Athens for safety. Eventually the Greeks gained the upper hand and drove the Persians out of their land.

The loss of the Greco-Persian Wars did little to hurt the Persian Empire, but it did much for the advancement of the Greeks. Even though they had

Western view of the Temple of Poseidon. The Greeks gave tribute to Poseidon after their victory over the Persians.

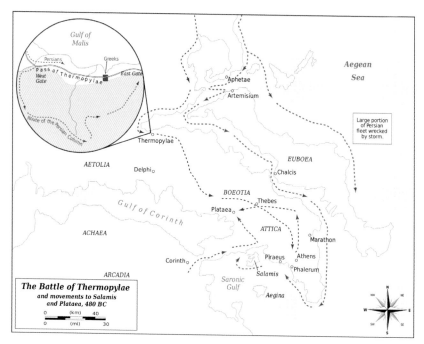

The Battle of Thermopylae and movements to Salamis and Plataea, 480 BC

many divisions and conflicts among their city-states, their struggle against a common enemy brought them together. This was one small step that showed the nation that unity was not out of the question. Nevertheless, unity was still many years away.

RESTORATION

War was not the only thing that marked this period of history, however. This epic century was also characterized by the great blessing of restoration.

The emergence of the Persian Empire on the world scene affected the beleaguered nation of Israel in a positive way. Under the reign of Cyrus, the Is-

raelites were able to return to Jerusalem and rebuild their city and temple. During the rebuilding process, however, some local enemies opposed the Israelites' efforts.

For more on the restoration of Israel, see Ezra and Nehemiah.

When the Assyrians conquered the northern kingdom of Israel, they had removed many of the Jews and forced them to live in other countries, and they had also forced people from other countries to live in Israel. Many of the Israelites who remained in the land intermarried with these other nations, and their descendants, whose ancestry and religion became mixed, came to be known as Samaritans.

When the Jews returned from exile, some Samaritans, remembering the Jewish part of their heritage, asked to help in the rebuilding of the temple. But the Jews refused to allow them. This clearly set the Samaritans at odds with the returning Jews.

■ *Now when the adversaries of Judah and Benjamin heard that the returned exiles were building a temple to the* LORD, *the God of Israel, they approached Zerubbabel and the heads of fathers' houses and said to them, "Let us build with you, for we worship your God as you do, and we have been sacrificing to him ever since the days of Esarhaddon king of Assyria who brought us here." But Zerubbabel, Jeshua, and the rest of the heads of fathers' houses in Israel said to them, "You have nothing to do with us in building a house to our God; but we alone will build to the* LORD, *the God of Israel, as King Cyrus the king of Persia has commanded us." Then the people of the land discouraged the people of Judah and made them afraid to build and bribed counselors against them to frustrate their purpose, all the days of Cyrus king of Persia, even until the reign of Darius king of Persia. And in the reign of Ahasuerus, in the beginning of his reign, they wrote an accusation against the inhabitants of Judah and Jerusalem (Ezra 4:1–6).*

This tension between the returning Jews and the Samaritans was very intense, and it became an obstacle to the rebuilding of the temple. Nehemiah

Monument of the Battle of Thermopylae

faced a similar tension when he led the efforts to rebuild the wall surrounding Jerusalem (Nehemiah 4:1–14). This conflict also motivated the prophets Haggai and Zechariah to hurry the people to get busy building the temple (Haggai 1:4–6; Zechariah 6:9–15).

It was also during this time that another popular story from the Bible occurred—the story of Esther. Esther 1:1 gives us the setting for this event:

■ *Now in the days of Ahasuerus, the Ahasuerus who reigned from India to Ethiopia over 127 provinces. . . (Esther 1:1).*

Above: This is the traditional mausoleum of Esther and Mordecai. It is located in Hamadan, Iran. Left: Artwork originally printed in Doré's English Bible. Artist: Gustave Doré (1832–1883).

The name Ahasuerus is understood to refer to King Xerxes, who ruled Persia at the peak of its power. It was his father, Darius, who expanded the empire until it was the largest kingdom in the history of the ancient world. Xerxes took the throne in 485 BC, and four years later tried to conquer Greece. It is during the period between his ascension to the throne and his attack on Greece that the story of Esther takes place.

THE STORY OF ESTHER IS, IN A CERTAIN SENSE, A VERY SIMPLE STORY, YET IT IS FILLED WITH MUCH DRAMA. THE STORY OPENS WITH AN ACCOUNT OF HOW XERXES DIVORCED HIMSELF FROM HIS QUEEN, VASHTI, AND BEGAN TO LONG FOR ANOTHER. HE WAS A VERY POWERFUL MAN, FOR HE RULED THE MOST POWERFUL EMPIRE IN THE WORLD. AS SUCH, HE WAS ABLE TO GET WHAT HE WANTED WHEN HE WANTED IT. HE ORDERED A SEARCH FOR THE MOST BEAUTIFUL GIRL IN HIS KINGDOM TO BE FOUND SO HE COULD MARRY HER. AFTER A LENGTHY SEARCH, A JEW NAMED ESTHER WAS CHOSEN. MORDECAI, HER UNCLE, ASKED HER NOT TO REVEAL TO ANYONE HER HERITAGE, WHICH ALSO MEANT THAT SHE WAS NOT TO REVEAL HER RELIGION.

Among Xerxes's advisers was a man named Haman, who was promoted by the king to a position of great importance in the kingdom. This was significant because Xerxes was planning to go to war with Greece and needed to leave a man in charge to run the kingdom in his absence. Haman convinced the king to order all to bow to him, but Mordecai refused to obey the order. This refusal angered Haman so much that he wanted not only to kill Mordecai but to destroy the entire Jewish race as well. So Haman tricked Xerxes into ordering the death of the Jewish people. When Mordecai read the order of the king to exterminate the Jews, he immediately went into mourning with sackcloth and ashes. The rest of the account tells how God used Esther to save the Jewish people from annihilation.

One of the amazing truths we learn from this story is God's ability to raise up just the right people at just the right time to accomplish His purposes. Xerxes, arguably the most powerful king on earth, was on the verge of launch-

The picture below is of Hamantaschen, which are filled pastries eaten during Purim. They are called "Haman's ears" in reference to the defeated enemy of the Jewish people.

ing into another war with his vast army. Yet through the faithful actions of two simple people, God was able to get Xerxes's attention and save Israel from destruction. That is why this event is remembered each year in Israel with the Feast of Purim. *Purim* means "lots," referring to Haman's casting of lots to determine what day the Jews were to be killed. However,

For more on the origins of Purim, see Esther 8.

God did not allow His children to be killed, but instead killed the aggressor. The God of Israel is more powerful than any king on earth.

One thing we observe in the process of Israel's return to the land is that, all along the way, it was not easy. Things were difficult and there were many obstacles. Yet God was with His people, and they were able to return. When things seemed dark and the nation was suffering the consequences of its rebellion, God, in His grace and mercy, was also restoring what had been destroyed. God did not allow any rebellion or sin to get in the way of His work.

REFORM

In addition to war and restoration, *reform* was another distinguishing characteristic of this pivotal century. In fact, during this time, both China and Greece underwent reforms so powerful that their impact is still felt today.

CHINA

Around the time that the people of Judah were living in exile in Babylon, China was suffering intense internal struggle. The nation endured continual warfare from several factions that were vying for control of the nation, and there seemed to be no end in sight to the constant fighting.

Out of this difficult tension, two men emerged who sought to understand and prevent war: Confucius and Sun Tzu. Their approaches to war, which are still studied today, differed greatly from each other. We will look at both to learn more about their lasting impact on Chinese culture and thinking.

Confucius

Confucius

In 551 BC, a boy by the name of Kong was born to a poor family in the province of

He was known to his disciples as Kong Fuzi, which means "Kong the master," but this became transliterated into Latin as "Confucius" when an Italian monk first introduced Kong's teaching to Europe.

Shandong. When Kong was three years old, his father died, leaving only his mother to raise him, which she did with great tenderness. From his earliest years, Kong displayed an extraordinary love of learning. He had a deep yearning and respect for the ancient laws of his country, which he studied intensely. As a child, Kong held religion in high regard; as a young adult, he earned a reputation for fairness and politeness.

After his mother died, Kong shut himself up in his house in a state of mourning for three years to honor her. During this time, he decided to devote himself to understanding the world around him and sought to understand even life and death. This led him to reflect deeply on the eternal laws of morality, and he struggled to find and understand the universal law that drives all other moral laws. His desire was to transform his mind with a sense of the responsibilities the moral laws impose upon all people. His goal was to understand these laws and create from them the unchangeable rule that would govern everything he did in life. As a result of this study, everything Kong did and taught ultimately found its source in his ethical reflections from this period of his life.

This plaque is on display at the Ritsumeikan University, Kyoto, Japan. It is a proverb that reads:
"What you know, you know, what you don't know, you don't know. This is true wisdom."

After that formative time of reflection, Kong's desire was to instruct his countrymen in the precepts of morality and all the virtues that derive from them. Over time, his teaching drew many disciples, as the practical nature of his philosophy became increasingly understood. He spent many years instructing his disciples in the foundations of his moral thinking. He was known to his disciples as Kong Fuzi, which means "Kong the master," but this became transliterated into Latin as "Confucius" when an Italian monk first introduced Kong's teaching to Europe.

During this time, the internal power struggles and conflicts within China resulted in hardships for the Chinese people. Confucius believed he could alleviate many of these troubles if he could rise to a position of influence and promote his ideas about morality. At one point, he held a governorship, but it was taken away. Instead, he spent much of his life wandering around China and teaching as many disciples as he could. Never in his lifetime did he reach his goal of affecting China's political system to bring about a revolution. One of his lasting contributions, however, was an ethical system of morality not tied to religious practice. In other words, he offered ethics without religion. For Confucius, ethics and morality were a universal law for all humanity that transcended religion.

Confucius taught several core values that he believed would put an end to wars and lead to prosperity if all people would embrace them:

- Li: ritual, propriety, etiquette
- Hsiao: love within the family—love of parents for their children and of children for their parents
- Yi: righteousness—the noblest way to act in any situation
- Xin: honesty and trustworthiness
- Jen: benevolence, humaneness toward others—the highest Confucian virtue
- Chung: loyalty to the state and authority

BY THE TIME CONFUCIUS DIED, HIS TEACHINGS HAD NOT PERVADED CHINESE SOCIETY IN THE WAY HE HAD ENVISIONED. YET LATER THEY TRULY DID CATCH ON AND HAD A SIGNIFICANT IMPACT ON CHINESE CULTURE. CONFUCIAN PHILOSOPHY BECAME ONE OF THE MOST WIDESPREAD IN ALL ASIA. HIS IDEAS LAID THE FOUNDATION IN CHINA FOR AN UNDERSTANDING OF HUMAN RIGHTS, INDIVIDUAL LIBERTY, AND DUE PROCESS OF LAW. EVEN TODAY, HIS IDEAS PLAY A MAJOR ROLE IN SHAPING THE SOCIETY OF CHINA. HOWEVER, THE ONE AREA IN WHICH HIS TEACHINGS WERE NEVER REALIZED WAS THE ENDING OF WAR.

Sun Tzu

Around the same time as Confucius, another political and moral philosopher arose. His name was Sun Tzu. According to traditional sources, Sun Tzu became a heroic general for the king of Wu, King Helü, and his military victories inspired him to write his master

Sun Tzu

work, *The Art of War.* The continual warfare among the seven provinces of China (Zhao, Qi, Qin, Chu, Han, Wei, and Yan), with each province seeking to control the entire kingdom, sapped the energy of the people. Many sought ways to put an end to these continual conflicts. It was Sun Tzu's conviction that the best way to stop a war is to win it. He believed that protracted warfare hurt the nation. Therefore, the goal should be to win a war as quickly as possible with power, force, and discipline.

When you engage in actual fighting, if victory is long in coming, the men's weapons will grow dull and their ardor will be dampened. If you lay siege to a town, you will exhaust your strength, and if the campaign is protracted, the resources of the state will not be equal to the strain. Never forget: when your weapons are dulled, your ardor dampened, your strength exhausted, and your treasure spent, other chieftains will spring up to take advantage of your extremity. Then no man, however wise, will be able to avert the consequences that must ensue.

In short, Sun Tzu believed that quick and decisive conquest—not passivity and moral benevolence—was the best way to deal with conflict. He also believed that if generals were allowed to lead the nation, order would be maintained, because soldiers are required to obey their officers without question, and this order would bring peace.

It is interesting to note the very different perspectives on war and peace that were held by Sun Tzu and Confucius. Sun Tzu believed that structure, order, discipline, and decisive victory were the best ways to bring about an end to political conflict. Confucius believed that there is a universal moral order that should govern everyone, and if people were taught this moral order, peace would be the result.

THE ART
OF WAR

Both men's philosophical convictions simply reinforce the Judeo-Christian belief that every person has been created in the image of God. Because God is moral and ethical in His very nature, mankind is always searching for some type of morality to govern society and for some way to put an end to conflict, which is actually a consequence of sin.

However, the answer to the world's problems is not to be found in an education of moral philosophy or in discipline and strength. The answer is found in the righteousness that is revealed from God. After the apostle Paul described the universal state of depravity that is in all people, he declared:

> ■ *But now the righteousness of God has been manifested apart from the law, although the Law and the Prophets bear witness to it (Romans 3:21).*

In the person and work of Jesus Christ, God has revealed His righteousness, which is available to all who trust in Jesus for salvation. This is the only hope for dealing with the depravity of the world.

China was not the only place where political and social reflection were under way. Greece was also going through philosophical reformation.

GREECE

After the Greeks pushed out the Persians around 480 BC, there was relative unity among the Greek city-states. This peace did not last long, however, for

This drawing is from a manuscript created ca. AD 1180. The seat of philosophy is pictured above. Underneath her are Socrates (left) and Plato (right).

in less than one generation, a conflict emerged from within that ravaged the Greek people.

Yet during this brief window of peace, often referred to as Greece's Golden Age, a man emerged whose impact was felt not only in Greek culture but also in the rest of the world for generations to come—even down to our own age. That man was Socrates.

Socrates was the first of three great Athenian philosophers, the other two being Plato and Aristotle. He was born in Athens in 469 BC, when the city was under the leadership of Pericles, a very powerful statesman, orator, and general.

Aristotle statue located at Stageira, Greece

Left: *The School of Athens* by Raffaello Sanzio (1510). This painting depicts Plato (left) and Aristotle (right).
Right: Medieval manuscript of a Latin translation of Aristotle's work.

Pericles, who himself was well educated, influenced the Athenians to pursue excellence in all learning.

Athens had a powerful navy. After the war with the Persians, they used their knowledge of ships and their war fleet to create a successful merchant armada that carried out extensive international trade. In contrast, Sparta reverted to an agrarian economy and began to sink into stagnation. During this time, a group of Athenian philosophers and sages called the Sophists began to emerge. These men strove to understand the world around them, the nature of the universe, the purpose of life, and other metaphysical ideas.

SOCRATES CAME OF AGE IN THIS ENVIRONMENT OF PEACE, FREEDOM, AND LEARNING, THOUGH HIS OWN ORIGINS WERE COMPARATIVELY HUMBLE. HIS FATHER WAS MOST LIKELY A STONE CARVER, AND IT IS BELIEVED THAT SOCRATES HIMSELF WORKED FOR A TIME IN THIS TRADE. HIS MOTHER WAS A MIDWIFE. SOCRATES, HOWEVER, DEVELOPED INTO A VERY DEEP THINKER AND PROVOCATIVE PHILOSOPHER. HE EVENTUALLY AMASSED A FOLLOWING OF DISCIPLES, ONE OF WHOM WAS THE FAMOUS PHILOSOPHER PLATO.

A Roman replica of the bust of Pericles

When the Peloponnesian War began in 431 BC, Socrates fought bravely for Athens. This war was a critical turning point both for the nation of Greece and in the life of Socrates.

The underlying cause of the war, according to the historian Thucydides, was the fear among the other Greek city-states of Athens's growing power. After the Persians had been driven out of Greece once and for all, Pericles did much to establish Athens. He made the Athenian navy one of the strongest in the world, established a defensive alliance with the city-state of Corcyra (Corinth's most bitter enemy), and renewed alliances with two cities to the west, Rhegium and Leontini. Even the food supply for much of Greece was in danger of coming under Athenian control.

With such advancements in Athens, the Greeks in the city of Corinth became afraid and sought help from Sparta to stop the Athenian develop-

The Tomb of the Unknown Soldier in Athens, Greece. This is a modern-day monument, but the inscriptions found here are from the Funeral Oration of Pericles in 430 BC.

ment. A coalition of anti-Athenian forces attacked Athens, and Socrates was among those who fought bravely to defend the city.

Athens eventually succumbed to the coalition, and the once-powerful city was practically reduced to a slave state for Sparta, the new leading power of Greece. The costs of the war were felt all across the country. Poverty became widespread, and the economic prosperity that once characterized Athens was gone.

This reversal of fortune deeply affected the life and work of Socrates. Prior to the war, the Sophists challenged the conventional notions of morality, religion, and human virtue. Much of Athenian philosophical thought focused on human freedom and autonomy, and less on adherence to serving the gods. After the loss of the Peloponnesian War, many in Athens began to long for the days when moral order was based on the traditional polytheistic religion of Greece. When Socrates was asked to weigh in on the issue, he instead encouraged them to continue their progressive thinking. Because of this, Socrates was charged with impiety and corruption of the youth. After Socrates's trial before an Athenian jury, he was convicted and sentenced to death. His sentence was carried out in a traditional manner—he was given a poisonous hemlock drink.

Socrates never wrote down any of his ideas while he was alive, because he himself was illiterate. But after he died, his student Plato recorded what Socrates had taught. One of Socrates's greatest contributions was his method of seeking truth. In the Socratic method, the primary role of the teacher is to ask provocative questions to prompt one's students to fully examine and understand what they believe to be true. In short, Socrates believed that truth is discovered better in dialogue than in the mere transmission of propositional ideas. Thus, he promoted what is sometimes called the analytical method of learning (also called the "Socratic method").

> Socrates never wrote down any of his ideas while he was alive, because he himself was illiterate. But after he died, his student Plato recorded what Socrates had taught.

However, while Socrates's continual pursuit of truth and his endless questioning of the assumptions of society drove some to a deeper understanding of the world around them, these same things drove others to hate him. Yet his approach to learning and his quest for understanding have continued to shape the lives of millions of people throughout history.

THE IMPACT OF GREEK CULTURE

The influence of Greek culture on the world is virtually immeasurable. It has left an indelible mark on politics, entertainment, medicine, architecture, and many other aspects of our lives. Below is just a sampling of the contributions the ancient Greeks made to the world:

1. *Medicine.* When we go to the doctor, we typically assume that the doctor is committed to making us healthy. Much of our confidence is rooted in the fact that all certified doctors in the United States are required to uphold

the Hippocratic Oath, by which they bind themselves to seek the good of their patients. Where did such an oath come from? Ancient Greece.

Hippocrates was born on the Greek island of Cos around the year 460 BC. According to tradition, he learned medicine from his father and grandfather, and he himself became a famous physician and teacher of medicine.

Hippocrates broke with the understanding of his day concerning the origin of sickness. Before Hippocrates, it was assumed that religion and medicine were closely linked.

Hippocrates broke with the understanding of his day concerning the origin of sickness. Before Hippocrates, it was assumed that religion and medicine were closely linked. Whenever someone became sick, the cause was assumed to be spiritual as well as physical; and thus the sick were given both a spiritual and physical (or medical) treatment. Hippocrates rejected the idea that illnesses were caused by the gods punishing disobedient followers. Instead, he believed that sickness was merely the product of environmental factors, diet, and unhealthy living habits. This doesn't mean that Hippocrates rejected the spiritual nature of the world. Instead, he simply looked beyond spiritual factors to uncover other sources of illness.

Either Hippocrates or one of his followers composed what is now widely known as the Hippocratic Oath, by which a doctor swears to regard the good of the patient and the preservation of life as overarching goals in all treatment. This oath is rooted in Hippocrates's foundational belief in the inherent value of human life, and his belief that physicians should hold to a high ethical standard in their practice of medicine. Hippocratic principles are still in use today in the West.

2. *Politics.* The first known democracy was established in Athens. The modern notions of political freedom, the right of all people to have a voice, the empowerment of the people, and the importance of limited government all find their roots in Athenian democracy.

3. *Education.* In addition to their earlier advancements in math and geometry, the Greeks made great contributions to the study of literature, drama, and philosophy. Many of the basic ideas they developed are still in use today, including the philosophical works of Socrates, Plato, and Aristotle.

From this brief overview of the contributions of ancient Greece to modern society, it is clear that our world today has been greatly shaped by Greek thought. Even the Greek language has played a role in shaping history—both sacred and secular. In the next chapter, we will examine the conquests of Alexander the Great and how he spread Greek thought and culture around the world.

Through the spread of the Greek language, God used Alexander to help disseminate the gospel throughout the entire Western and Near Eastern world. As Greek became a somewhat universal language, it helped everyone to communicate and to easily gain access to the written Word of God. By the time the apostles began to spread the news of Jesus' death, burial, and resurrection, they could do so in a language that most literate people could read, no matter where they lived in the Roman Empire.

Alexander the Great

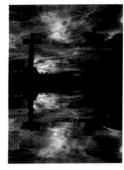

REFLECTIONS

The catalog of events that occurred during this pivotal period of one hundred years is nothing short of incredible. During this era, we see God doing some remarkable things:

1. Keeping His word. God said that the Jews would return to the land, and they did. God moved the heart of a leader to bring this about.

2. Protecting His children. God did not allow the Jews to be wiped out by those who opposed them. God raised up Esther to a place of significant influence, from which she was able to thwart the wicked plans of an evil man.

3. Advancing His kingdom. God allowed Greek culture to lay a foundation that would later be used to spread the gospel to the world.

Our God is sovereign over all history—secular, sacred, and redemptive. This should give us hope and strength. God is at work even if we do not see it. He is moving the hearts of kings; therefore, there is nothing to fear. No one can stop God and His plan for the world.

TIME LINE
500 BC – 400 BC

BIBLE EVENT   **WORLD EVENT**

516—Jewish temple is completed

500

492–479—Greco-Persian Wars
485—Xerxes I begins reign in Persia

478—Esther becomes queen

469—Birth of Socrates
464—Artaxerxes reigns in Persia
461—Peloponnesian War

465—Malachi begins ministry

457—Ezra sent to Judah

450—Joel begins ministry

450

444—Nehemiah sent to Judah

441—Euripides writes his first play

431—Peloponnesian War renewed

404—Artaxerxes II reigns in Persia

400

All dates are approximate.

CHAPTER 7

ESTABLISHMENT, CONFLICT, AND DOMINATION

THE SILENT YEARS
400–1 BC

Many years ago, a popular poem captured the hearts of many people and brought comfort to millions. The poem eventually became so popular that an entire industry of products was built around it—including songs, greeting cards, wall hangings, coffee mugs, and T-shirts. The poem, titled "Footprints in the Sand," tells of a night when the poet dreamed about walking along the seashore with Jesus. At some points along the way, two sets of footprints were visible in the sand; but at other, more difficult times, only one set of footprints was visible. When the poet asked Jesus why He seemed to be absent during her times of greatest need, He replied, "During the times when you saw only one set of footprints, those were times when I carried you."

The poem was written in 1936 by a young woman named Mary Stevenson. She wrote the poem to remind people that even though it appears at times that we're alone, the reality is that Jesus is always with us. Sometimes His work in our lives is invisible, but this does not mean He is any less

present or powerful. Often, when it appears God is absent, He is actually the most present, carrying us through the troubled times.

God's constant presence is an important truth to keep in mind as we enter into the period of history that some have called the Silent Years—a span of four hundred years during which it appears God stopped speaking to Israel. Though history continues to roll along through the years, it seems that sacred and redemptive history were put on hold. To some, it seems as if God's very presence in the world was withdrawn for four centuries.

TRANSITION FROM THE
GREEKS TO THE ROMANS

During this time, Israel and the world were shaken with all kinds of wars and strife. During these so-called Silent Years, many important events took place that would greatly affect God's purposes in the world. The end of these Silent Years is marked by the entrance of God Himself into the world through a miracle that is bigger than anyone could have ever imagined.

In this chapter, we will take a closer look at the Greek Empire and the transition from the Greeks to the Romans. This will help us understand

Ruins of the Temple of Zeus in Athens, Greece. The pillar on its side collapsed in 1852.

Bust of Alexander the Great. This sculpture is a copy of a bronze sculpture made by Lysippos. This copy was found in Tivoli, east of Rome.

some very important events that shaped not only sacred and redemptive history but also secular history for centuries. To begin this journey, we will look at one of the most powerful figures of this time, Alexander the Great, and the important influence he had on secular and sacred history.

ALEXANDER THE GREAT

At the end of chapter 6, we looked briefly at how several advancements in Greek culture affected the fields of medicine, politics, and education. What we did not address was how these advancements made their way from Greece to the other nations of the world.

After the Peloponnesian War, Athens was left in a state of disrepair. Because of the many soldiers who were killed in battle, the city was filled with many widows and fatherless children. In addition, the once prosperous city was left in economic ruin without much hope for recovery. The people were not able to sustain enough agricultural activity to provide sufficient food for everyone.

Sparta was only slightly better off. Though they had been victorious in the war, while they were fighting they had neglected their farms, leaving the population without enough food. In addition, many of their vineyards and fruit-bearing trees had been destroyed in the war, which also contributed to the shortage of food.

IN SHORT, THE ENTIRE COUNTRY WAS SUFFERING THE EFFECTS OF POSTWAR DESTRUCTION. DUE TO THE DIFFICULT LIVING CONDITIONS AT HOME, MANY SPARTAN SOLDIERS LEFT GREECE TO BECOME MERCENARIES FOR THE PERSIANS. FOR SOLDIERS WHO HAD KNOWN NOTHING BUT FIGHTING FOR CLOSE TO THIRTY YEARS, CONTINUING TO FIGHT SEEMED THE MOST LOGICAL WAY TO PROVIDE FOR THEIR FAMILIES IN SUCH ECONOMIC STRESS.

As bad as things were for Greece, God was not yet finished with this nation. As unlikely as it may have seemed at this point in history, God made it clear through the prophecy of Daniel that the Greeks would eventually conquer the Persian Empire and become the new rulers of the world (Daniel 2:39). But how would Greece ever resurface from the political and economic pit into which it had descended as a result of the Peloponnesian War? For the answer to this question, we must shift our attention to Macedonia, a region located in the northern part of the Grecian peninsula.

The people of Macedonia were considered barbaric by the rest of the Greek population, who paid little attention to them. Yet out of this neglected region, a ruler emerged by the name of Philip, who turned the men of Macedonia into a powerful fighting force. He amassed a great army and—through much discipline and training—exerted his control over the rest of Greece, uniting the entire peninsula for the first time in history.

However, Philip had his eye on something bigger than just a unified Greece: he wanted to conquer Persia, the reigning superpower of his time. But before he was able to muster his army to move into Persia, Philip was murdered, leaving his dream to be fulfilled by his son Alexander III, whom we know today as Alexander the Great. Alexander would not only fulfill his father's dream of conquering the Persian Empire, but far surpass it by spreading Greek culture throughout the world.

Alexander was born in 356 BC, and when he turned thirteen years old, his father hired the famous Greek philosopher Aristotle to be Alexander's personal tutor. During the next three years, Aristotle trained Alexander in rhetoric and literature, and

King Philip II of Macedonia

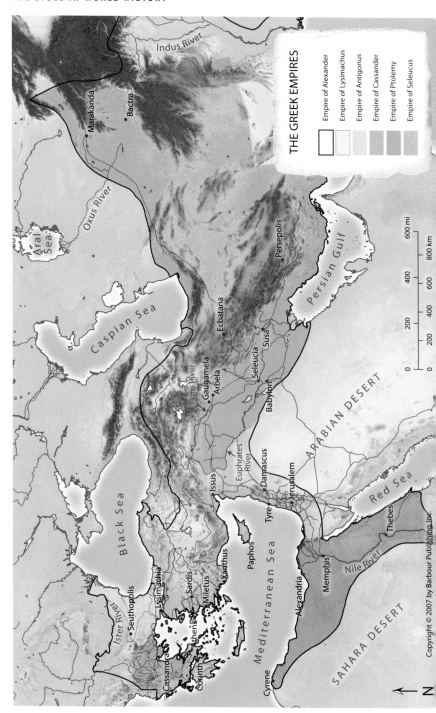

THE GREEK EMPIRES

Empire of Alexander
Empire of Lysimachus
Empire of Antigonus
Empire of Cassander
Empire of Ptolemy
Empire of Seleucus

Indus River

Marakanda

Bactra

Oxus River

Aral Sea

Caspian Sea

Persepolis

Persian Gulf

Ecbatana

Susa

Seleucia

Gaugamela

Arbela

Babylon

Tigris River

ARABIAN DESERT

Euphrates River

Issus

Damascus

Jerusalem

Tyre

Red Sea

Black Sea

Thebes

Paphos

Xanthus

Memphis

Nile River

Sardis

Miletus

Athens

Alexandria

Ister River

Seuthopolis

Lysimachia

SAHARA DESERT

Mediterranean Sea

Cyrene

Cassandra

Corinth

600 mi

800 km

400

600

200

400

200

0

0

N

Copyright © 2007 by Barbour Publishing, Inc.

stimulated his interest in science, medicine, and philosophy. Alexander became convinced that the best way to live was the "Greek way," and he envisioned a world in which all the people he conquered would be taught Greek ways of thinking and living. He believed that if people embraced Greek culture, they would never want to leave that way of life and would forever embrace his empire.

After Philip died, Alexander acted quickly to take control of his father's troops,

> # After Philip died, Alexander acted quickly to take control of his father's troops, quell the rebellions that had erupted, and maintain control of the nation.

quell the rebellions that had erupted, and maintain control of the nation. Now with a unified country behind him and a strong fighting force in front of him, Alexander turned his attention to his father's unmet desire, the conquering of Persia.

In 334 BC Alexander led his army of 42,000 troops into Asia and began to slowly and systematically take over the Persian Empire one province at a time. By 323, the year of his death, Alexander had conquered the entire Persian Empire, bringing to fruition the vision that God showed Nebuchadnezzar in Daniel 2:39.

True to his convictions, as Alexander conquered nation after nation, he spread the Greek language, culture, and writing system all over the known world. This initiated a worldwide process that has come to be called Hellenization, from the Greek word *Hellas*, meaning "Greece."

Because of Alexander's actions, Greek became one of the most universal languages of this period. Greek logic, philosophy, and education became the standard throughout Asia and the Middle East. This had a major impact on sacred history. Because much of the world was familiar with a common language, by the time of the New Testament, the apostles were able to record the events of Jesus in a language that virtually all literate people in the Roman Empire would be able to read and understand.

This page of the Greek New Testament is from a collection of fragments called "Papyrus 46" (or P46). This page contains 2 Corinthians 11:33–12:9. In its entirety, P46 is one of the most complete early editions of the New Testament.

THE WORLD AFTER ALEXANDER

After Alexander conquered the Persian Empire, it seemed as if nothing could stop the young warrior. However, it was not the will of God that Alexander would rule the world for long. Even though Alexander wanted to continue his path of conquest by making his way into India, his men were exhausted and refused to fight further. Soon after this, Alexander developed a high fever after attending a private party at the home of a friend.

The fever became stronger with each succeeding day, to the point where Alexander was unable to move or speak. At this point, his advisers knew that he was about to die, so they allowed the Macedonians to file past their leader one last time before he finally succumbed to the illness. Alexander the Great, the Macedonian king and great conqueror of the Persian Empire, died at the age of thirty-three without designating a successor to his empire.

At the time of Alexander's death, his son was too young to take the throne. Therefore, a regent was placed in charge of the boy, and Alexander's great empire was divided into five regions, to be ruled by the regent and four of Alexander's top generals. This division of territory led to great conflict over many years (until about 30 BC), as the five rulers fought to expand their own regions and take land from the other leaders. Thus, Alexander's great empire quickly disintegrated into several smaller empires that constantly vied for power.

Marble bust of Ptolemy I Soter, king of Egypt (305–282 BC). Ptolemy was the founder of the Ptolemaic dynasty. Inset: Ptolemy and his wife Eurydice.

Two particular powers that arose from Alexander's great empire are significant for understanding sacred and redemptive history. The first was Alexander's former general Ptolemy, who controlled the region of Egypt. At some point during his reign, he conferred upon himself the title of Soter, which means "savior." Ptolemy was a strong proponent of Hellenization and established his capital at Alexandria in northern Egypt.

In Alexandria he founded a museum and started collecting books for a library, which, under his successors, became a center for scientific research and the best collection of Greek and Roman papyri in the world. As sailors came into Alexandria for commerce, Ptolemy's scribes asked to borrow whatever scrolls they had on their ships. The scribes would then copy the scrolls to add to the library.

Papyrus plant (inset) used to make a papyrus for scribes. This ancient papyrus is an old Egyptian record of the royal tombs.

Ptolemy also built one of the Seven Wonders of the Ancient World: the lighthouse on the island of Pharos, off the coast of Alexandria. This immense lighthouse enabled ships to navigate their way to Alexandria at night and in all sorts of weather.

The Seven Wonders of the Ancient World (from left to right, top to bottom): Great Pyramid of Giza, Hanging Gardens of Babylon, Temple of Artemis, Statue of Zeus at Olympia, Mausoleum of Maussollos, Colossus of Rhodes, and Lighthouse of Alexandria. All paintings are by a Dutch artist named Martin Heemskerck who lived between 1498 and 1574.

During Ptolemy's reign, many Jews migrated to Alexandria from Israel. Over time, Jewish migration grew to such an extent that, at its zenith, 40 percent of the population was Jewish. As the process of Hellenization took hold, many of these expatriate Jews were no longer familiar with Hebrew, the language of scripture. Therefore, the need emerged for the Hebrew scriptures to be translated into Greek. According to tradition, seventy trusted scribes translated the Hebrew text into Greek. This translation of the scriptures is commonly called the Septuagint, from the Greek word for "seventy."

The translation of Hebrew books into Greek did not stop with the thirty-nine books of the Old Testament. Other books such as Tobit, Sirach, Judith, and 1 and 2 Maccabees were also translated. These and other books outside the canon of the Old Testament are commonly known as the Apocrypha.

PTOLEMY SOTER'S RULE OVER EGYPT LASTED FROM 332 TO 283 BC. PTOLEMY'S SON, PTOLEMY II PHILADELPHOS, CO-RULED FOR THE LAST TWO YEARS OF HIS FATHER'S REIGN AND THEN SUCCEEDED HIM. PTOLEMY I SOTER'S DYNASTY CONTINUED UNBROKEN UNTIL THE FAMOUS QUEEN CLEOPATRA LOST HER POWER OVER EGYPT TO THE ROMANS.

The Reign of the Seleucids

The other Greek power that was highly significant for sacred and redemptive history is the Seleucid Empire. Seleucus (358–280 BC) ruled over the old Persian Empire (minus Egypt), ranging from India to Turkey and from Ararat to Israel. Though it subsumed much of the infrastructure of the Persian Empire, the Seleucid Empire was another bastion of Greek culture. The Seleucids built hundreds of cities based on the Greek polis model, complete with gymnasiums, amphitheaters, and squares. And members of the up-

This first- or second-century marble sculpture is of Seleucus I Nicator. He was the Macedonian officer of Alexander the Great and founded the Seleucid Empire.

per classes became thoroughly Hellenistic in their customs and thinking.

Unlike Alexandria in Egypt, however, the Seleucid Empire never really established a notable center of Hellenistic learning. In this war-plagued region, successive kings struggled constantly to maintain their rule against others who sought to undermine their reign. This region also suffered attacks from other Greek powers—such as the Ptolemaic Empire—that wanted to expand their control.

In 175 BC a Seleucid leader who rose to power became notorious for his eccentric behavior as well as for his hatred of the Jews. His name was Antiochus IV Epiphanes (175–164 BC). Up to this point, the land of Israel had been fought over repeatedly by the Ptolemies and the Seleucids,

Antiochus IV

with the Ptolemies controlling the area most of the time. Around 175 BC, however, Israel was seized by the Seleucids, though their empire was losing territory elsewhere.

Antiochus also invaded Egypt, marching his army to Alexandria and laying siege to the city. The rising Roman Empire, however, sought to keep the Seleucid Empire from becoming too powerful by demanding that Antiochus withdraw from his siege. Wanting to keep peace with the Romans, Antiochus retreated from his attack. As he returned from Egypt, he marched up the coastline and took his frustration out on the regions of Israel and Syria.

In an effort to solidify his grip over his lands and prevent any defection, Antiochus instituted a strict policy of Hellenization throughout his empire. He made a furious and determined effort to exterminate the Jewish religion. He occupied Jerusalem (168 BC), defiled the temple, offered a pig on its altar, erected an altar to Jupiter, prohibited temple worship, forbade circumcision, sold thousands of Jewish families into slavery, destroyed all the copies of scripture he could find, slaughtered everyone who had the scriptures in their possession, and tortured the Jews with the hope of having them renounce their religion. In order to replenish his own coffers, he raided the temple in Jerusalem and stole all the gold and silver furnishings. This was a very dark moment in history for the people of Israel.

The desecration of the temple and other atrocities led to the Maccabean revolt, one of the most heroic feats in history. According to Jewish tradition, Antiochus sent Syrian overseers and soldiers to villages throughout Judea to enforce the edicts that required Jews to engage in pagan sacrifices and idol worship. When the Syrian soldiers reached Modiin, a town about seventeen miles northwest of Jerusalem, they demanded that the local leader, Mattathias, set

Above: *Sacrilege of Antiochus.* This engraving was first published in 1815 in London by P. J. De Loutherbourg.
Right: *Mattathias and the Apostate,* engraved by Gustave Doré (1832–1883)

> Mattathias killed not only the Jew who stepped forward to sacrifice the pig but also the king's representative. Then Mattathias cried out, "Whoever is for God, follow me!"

an example for his people by sacrificing a pig on a pagan altar. Mattathias, a member of the priestly class, refused to perform the sacrifice. However, another Jew stepped up to kill the pig. At this point, Mattathias killed not only the Jew who stepped forward to sacrifice the pig but also the king's representative. Then Mattathias cried out, "Whoever is for God, follow me!" Mattathias and his five sons fled to the Samarian hills and banded together to take back their land, the city of Jerusalem, and the temple of the Lord.

Mattathias was joined by a band of others like him, simple farmers armed only with bows and arrows, spears, and rocks, but passionately dedicated to the laws of Moses. They fought a guerilla war against the well-trained, well-equipped, seemingly endless forces of the mercenary Syrian army. Mattathias and his followers were called Maccabees, a name derived from a nickname (meaning "hammerer" or perhaps "hammerhead") given to Judas, one of Mattathias's sons, who took command of the troops after Mattathias died.

The Maccabees fought their way back to the Temple Mount, cleansed the temple, removed the defiled altar, and constructed a new one in its place. It took three years for the Maccabees to fully reclaim the temple. After their conquest, the Maccabees held a dedication of the temple. At this dedication, proper sacrifices were made, and the golden menorah was lit, followed by eight days of celebration and praise to God. This celebration, called the Feast of Dedication, or Hanukkah, is still observed by Jews today.

AS WE WILL SEE LATER, THE RISE OF ROME SIGNALED THE DEATH KNELL FOR THE GREEK KINGDOMS. MACEDONIA AND GREECE WERE CONQUERED IN 167 AND 145 BC, RESPECTIVELY, AND SELEUCID ASIA BY 65 BC. CLEOPATRA VII, THE LAST MACEDONIAN DESCENDANT OF PTOLEMY, COMMITTED SUICIDE IN 30 BC, AFTER WHICH EGYPT WAS ADDED TO THE ROMAN EMPIRE AS WELL.

THE ADVANCEMENT OF TRADE

We are going to take a step away from Greece and Rome for a moment and take a brief look at another significant development taking place throughout the world during this time.

Around 202 BC, a trade route known as the Silk Road came into prominent use, connecting people from China, India, Tibet, Persia, and the Mediterranean to an extent previously unknown in history. This "road" was not actually a single road, but a network of smaller routes that were already in use by traders, merchants, pilgrims, missionaries, soldiers, and other travelers.

The development of this network of roads significantly opened up trading between the Far East and the rest of the world. However, more than just the economy was affected by these routes, for they brought cultures and religions into contact with each other as never before. It was through the Silk Road that Buddhism spread to China from Nepal and India. Many people from the Mediterranean were exposed to Chinese culture for the first time, and vice versa. In a sense, the Silk Road was an ancient form of the Internet, opening communication between far-flung cultures and exposing people to previously unknown parts of the world.

The Silk Road also exposed people to some other things that were not so good. Wars were fought over control of the trade routes as the potential for

> The Silk Road did much to bring stability to the world and allowed cultures to flourish and grow as they positively interacted with others outside their own realms.

wealth became apparent. Disease also became more rampant as societies came into contact with each other for the first time and new illnesses spread to people who had not yet developed immunities to them. Nevertheless, in spite of all the negatives, it could be argued that the Silk Road did much to bring stability to the world and allowed cultures to flourish and grow as they positively interacted with others outside their own realms.

THE RISE OF ROME

Historians often view the rise of Rome in three stages. Stage 1 covers the period from about 3000 to 500 BC, when Rome was still emerging as a distinct power. Stage 2 covers the period of the Roman Republic from about 500 to 30 BC. Stage 3 covers the period of the Roman Empire, roughly 30 BC to AD 476. In this chapter, we will look at Stage 2, the period of the Roman Republic.

The Roman Republic began about the same time that democracy was getting started in Athens, when Roman aristocrats rebelled against the Etruscan kings who had ruled Rome for some time. The Etruscans were a group of

This Etruscan sarcophagus is dated between 550 and 500 BC.

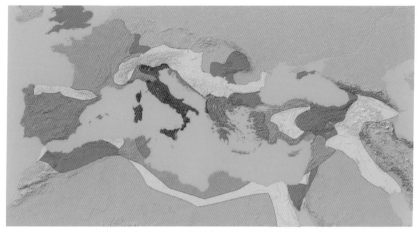

Extent of the Roman Empire in 218 BC (dark red), 133 BC (light red), 44 BC (orange), AD 14 (yellow), later acquisitions (green), and Trajan's Eastern conquests (light green)

people who migrated to the northern part of what is now Italy and ruled the region starting around 700 BC. The kings were fair, but they ruled mainly in favor of the poor and greatly taxed the rich. The aristocrats wanted to rid Rome of these kings, but they did not have the military resources to do so. Instead, they promised the poor that they could have power in the new government if they would help get rid of the kings. The poor agreed to help, and together they threw out the Etruscan kings. This was the start of what is called the Roman Republic.

Once the kings were ousted, the aristocrats failed to deliver on their promise of power to the poor, and the poor revolted. They put pressure on the rich by going on strike and stopping the economic production of the nation. Their tactic worked, and the new leadership in Rome gave the poor the right to vote—with the exception of slaves and women.

Rome did not have a direct democracy as Athens did, but instead it had a representative democracy, much like the United States. In this system, the poor voted for members of the aristocratic class to represent them. However, this system made the poor feel as if their interests were still not being fully addressed, because their representatives were not really chosen from among them. To address this issue, the Roman senate allowed the poor to elect tribunes from among their own people. The tribunes were given the right to veto any bill that they believed was not in the best interests of the poor. In addition, the poor required the senate to write down every bill and post it for all to read. This allowed the people to know what was being voted on so they could share their thoughts with the tribunes. These and other political developments shaped Rome's government in a way that allowed it to expand and thrive for many centuries. It also became the political foundation for the

These bronze doors once stood in the ancient Roman senate. These doors were taken from the Roman forum and restored in 1660 when they were placed in the Papal Archbasilica of St. John Lateran.

democratic movements that would emerge in the eighteenth and nineteenth centuries of the modern era.

While these developments were under way, the Roman army gradually conquered the surrounding cities. Their approach to conquest and empire building was unique in the ancient world up to that time. When they conquered a city, they fully integrated that city into their empire. All the men were given the right to vote, the city was allowed to create a tribune for the senate, and the people were granted all the benefits of the government. In addition, all the eligible men of the city were enrolled in the army, thereby allowing the Roman army to grow and conquer more cities. Through this process, the Roman Republic became stronger, richer, and more capable of expanding.

The Punic Wars

By 274 BC the Romans had taken over the entire Italian peninsula. Yet all was not perfect in Rome. To the south lay an island called Sicily. Half the island was controlled by the Greeks, and the other half was controlled by Carthage (modern Tunisia), a growing power in North Africa. The Romans sent troops to Sicily to attack the Greek half of the island, but the Carthaginians went on the offensive and attacked the Romans. This started a series of wars between the Romans and

the Carthaginians called the Punic Wars. The term *Punic* comes from the Latin name for the Carthaginians (*Punici* or *Poenici*), who were of Phoenician ancestry. Three Punic wars were fought over the span of about one hundred years and ended with Rome's clear victory over the Carthaginians.

During the Punic Wars, a Carthaginian general named Hannibal established himself as one of the greatest military leaders of all time. Hannibal's father was the leading Carthaginian commander during the First Punic War. One of Hannibal's most well-known triumphs occurred at the outbreak of the Second Punic War. He marched an army, including war elephants, from Iberia (modern Spain) over the Pyrenees and the Alps and into northern Italy—a feat that most would have said was impossible. He was very successful against Rome and won many victories; but eventually the Roman leaders learned his tactics and defeated him.

After the war, Hannibal successfully ran for office in Carthage and won. He enacted many reforms to help pay the war taxes that Rome had levied on

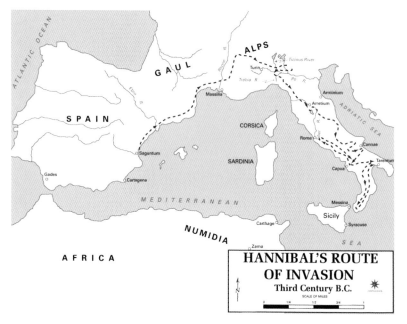

HANNIBAL'S ROUTE OF INVASION

Third Century B.C.

the city. However, his reforms were very unpopular with members of both the Carthaginian aristocracy and Rome, and he chose to leave Carthage. During his exile, he found refuge in the Seleucid court and acted as a military adviser to Antiochus III in his war against Rome. When Antiochus lost, Hannibal fled again, finding refuge in various cities before he was finally betrayed and placed in Roman custody.

Though Hannibal spent the remaining years of his life in a Roman jail, he is still considered one of the world's great military strategists, and his strategies and tactics were often adopted by his enemies.

Hannibal counting the rings of the Roman knights killed at the Battle of Cannae (216 BC). This marble statue was carved in 1704 by Sébastien Slodtz.

From Republic to Empire

By 146 BC the Romans controlled most of the coastline of the western Mediterranean Sea, leaving them as the only superpower in the region. However, this did not mean that everything was going smoothly for Rome. The republic was suffering from intense civil unrest.

> Rome struggled to rule its emerging empire with fairness. One contributing factor to Rome's troubles was the manner of their class distinctions.

Rome struggled to rule its emerging empire with fairness. One contributing factor to Rome's troubles was the manner of their class distinctions. In Rome, freemen could be drafted into military service, but slaves were exempt. Slaves also did not pay taxes, while freemen did. Rome's constant warfare meant that men were continually called to fight. As these men returned home, many found that their farms had been poorly kept. And because many of the men had become disabled, their debts went unpaid. Yet all the while, the merchants—who were part of the ruling class, and thus not sent to fight—expanded their wealth by exploiting trade routes opened up through warfare and also by foreclosing on the debt-ridden farms of the freemen who were sent to fight the wars. In addition, when the freemen returned from the war, the wealthy landowners would not hire them, because freemen were always eligible for military service again. Instead, the landowners purchased more slaves to do the work, because slaves could not be drafted.

This mosaic from the second century AD portrays Roman slaves.

This social and economic inequity led a man by the name of Tiberius Sempronius Gracchus to take up the cause of the poorer classes of Rome. His plan was to get laws passed that would protect the land of the soldiers and allow them to return to their farms without facing taxes and the fear of losing their homes due to mounting debts. The Roman senate, made up mainly of wealthy landowners, did not want any reform to the laws that would give tax breaks to the poorer classes; therefore, they opposed Tiberius's ideas. In the end, after a long, hard battle with the senate, Tiberius was killed in order to silence him once and for all.

Another conflict occurred over voting. Many citizens throughout Italy felt that Rome was not treating them fairly and wanted greater voting rights in the senate. This led to a

Warrior leaning on his spear while remembering his comrades who have fallen. The snake often symbolized the soul of the dead.

civil war—though, in the end, little political reform came about because of it.

Through all this social unrest, it became clear that the Roman senate was no longer capable on its own to run the emerging Roman Empire. People be-

gan to look for a single leader who would be able to hold the nation together. At this point, three powerful men of the empire joined forces: Pompey, Crassus, and Julius Caesar. Among these three, called the triumvirate, there seemed to be enough shared power to run the emerging empire. But the trio did not last long together; Crassus was killed in battle, which led Pompey and Julius Caesar to enter into a civil war against each other. Eventually Caesar won and Pompey fled to Egypt, but the Egyptians killed him to court favor with Caesar.

While Caesar was in Egypt to confirm the death of Pompey, he met Cleopatra and took her back to Rome. Later they had a child together. Now that Caesar had total con-

Bust of Marcus Licinius Crassus

trol of the empire and was also developing strong relations with Egypt, he proudly named himself dictator for life. This proved too great a threat to the power of the Roman senate, and they had Julius Caesar assassinated in 44 BC. Soon after this, Cleopatra developed a relationship with one of Caesar's friends, Mark Antony, and they had three children together. This popular story has been immortalized in film and literature.

Soon another group of men formed a second triumvirate: Mark Antony, Lepidus, and Octavian (Caesar's nephew and adopted son). However, sharing power among three people is very difficult for strong leaders, and eventually Lepidus was forced out of power. After this, Antony and Octavian entered into a civil war against

Above: Cleopatra and Caesarion. Back side of the Temple of Dendera. Caesarion was named after Julius Caesar and may have been his son. Right: Full-size image is bronze statue of Caesar (Rimini, Italy). The top right bust is housed in the Vatican Museums. The middle right image is an eighteenth-century sculpture that rests in the Summer Garden of Saint Petersburg. The bottom right image is an ancient bust of the emperor. The near right image is a statue that sits outside the Austrian Parliament.

JULIUS CAESAR

CLEOPATRA

each other. In 31 BC Octavian defeated Antony, who, along with Cleopatra, killed himself. This brought Egypt under the control of the Roman Empire, ending the last vestige of the Greek Empire spawned by Alexander the Great and his military campaigns.

THE FIGHT OVER ISRAEL

While Antony and Octavian fought for control of Rome, Israel faced a fight of its own. An Idumean (a descendant of the Edomites) named Herod, who would later be called Herod the Great, had been appointed as ruler over the small region of Galilee. When the Parthians, who controlled much of the former territory of the Seleucid Empire, invaded Palestine around 40 BC, Herod fled to Rome and was appointed king over Israel by the Roman senate, although technically he was more like a governor. Herod then returned to Galilee and fought many bitter battles to take possession of his kingdom.

Top: This coin with the image of Octavian was circulated ca. 30 BC.
Bottom: Mark Antony

As Herod took over as leader of Israel, he developed a number of adversaries—including the Jewish people themselves, and especially many of the religious leaders. They objected to both his ethnicity, since he was only half Jewish, and his friendship with the Romans. Though Herod was born in Jericho, he was not fully committed to the law of God, and his lineage was not regarded as giving him a legitimate claim to be king over Israel.

The second group of Herod's adversaries consisted of members of the nobility. Herod executed forty-five of the wealthiest people in Israel and confiscated their properties simply to increase his own wealth. This demonstrated that he would stop at nothing to establish his own power and wealth in the world.

The third group of Herod's adversaries consisted of his wife and her family. Herod married a Jewish woman descended from the Maccabees, who were widely regarded as the legitimate heirs to the throne of Israel. Herod's wife wanted him to name her brother, Aristobulus, as the high priest of Israel. Herod did so even though Aristobulus was only sixteen years old. After officiating a successful Feast of Tabernacles, Aristobulus became well loved by the people. This drove Herod into a state of extreme paranoia, because his

Left: Full-size image is Cleopatra VII committing suicide. Marble. Late seventeenth century by Claude Bertin. Top and middle left images are from the 1917 film titled *Cleopatra* starring Theda Bara (Cleopatra) and Fritz Leiber (Caesar). Bottom left image is of Caesar placing Cleopatra on the throne of Egypt. Painted in the 1630s by Pietro da Cortona.

own brother-in-law, who had a legitimate claim to the throne, now had the growing support of the people as well. So Herod invited Aristobulus to his house, where he "accidentally" drowned in the pool. People widely believed, however, that Herod had killed his brother-in-law.

For more on King Herod, read Matthew 2.

Herod's dealings with Aristobulus generated tension with more than just his wife. The mother of Herod's wife became angry, and so did the famous Egyptian queen Cleopatra, who was a close friend of Herod's mother-in-law. For this reason, Herod's actions led to tension between Egypt and Israel, and caused Herod to become even more paranoid and worried that his throne was going to be taken away.

Still, not everything was bad for Herod. As he solidified his throne, he enjoyed a period of prosperity for about thirteen years. In honor of Caesar, he introduced Olympic-style games and built amphitheaters throughout Israel.

Herod also rebuilt many fortresses in the land and even funded temples in Gentile territories. He built an elaborate royal palace for himself in Jerusalem as well as one in Jericho. According to the historian Josephus, however, Herod's most notable achievement was the building of a new temple in Je-

Roman theater, Caesarea, Israel

rusalem to replace the aging temple that had been built after the Jews returned from Babylonian exile. Herod's temple was begun in 20 or 19 BC and finished in AD 63, long after his death. In praise of the magnificent structure, the Jewish rabbis are recorded as saying, "He who has not seen the temple of Herod has never seen a beautiful building."

It was around this time that Herod reduced the taxes on the people by a third and made some very strong political and economic moves to increase the economy of Israel. Even though Herod was considered irreligious, his economic achievements brought great prosperity to Israel, which raised his esteem among the Jews considerably.

> Even though Herod was considered irreligious, his economic achievements brought great prosperity to Israel, which raised his esteem among the Jews considerably.

Ancient Roman amphitheater at Caesarea Maritima, Israel

UNFORTUNATELY, ALL GOOD THINGS MUST COME TO AN END. HEROD'S PROSPERITY LED TO DOMESTIC PROBLEMS THAT LASTED FOR ABOUT TEN YEARS. HE HAD ACQUIRED TEN WIVES, AND EACH WANTED HER SON OR SONS TO SUCCEED HIM. THUS, HIS FAMILY LIFE BEGAN TO TAKE A MAJOR TOLL ON HIS SANITY. THIS STRESS WAS SO GREAT THAT HE BEGAN TO MURDER ANYONE—EVEN HIS OWN FAMILY—WHO MIGHT POTENTIALLY THREATEN HIS POSITION AS KING. HEROD'S PARANOIA SEEMED TO INCREASE FOR THE REST OF HIS LIFE UNTIL HE HAD MURDERED VIRTUALLY EVERYONE WHO WAS EVER CLOSE TO HIM.

This picture of a paranoid Herod fits perfectly with Matthew's account of Jesus' birth, which came near the end of Herod's life, and of Herod's attempt to eliminate Jesus by killing all the baby boys in Bethlehem. No matter how powerful Herod was as king, ultimately he could do nothing to thwart God's will and the advance of His kingdom.

Massacre of the Innocents by Duccio di Buoninsegna.
This painting was created between 1308 and 1311.

THE BIRTH OF JESUS:
THE ARRIVAL OF THE KING OF KINGS

The birth of Jesus came at a very intense time for the world. The Roman Empire, which controlled most of the Mediterranean world, had just emerged from a civil war that resulted in its transformation from a republic to an empire. Israel in particular was still enduring the murderous paranoia that plagued Herod the Great in his last days. Given this backdrop, let us look at how the various people in the world reacted to the divine intersection of secular, sacred, and redemptive history. For the most part, they responded to Jesus' arrival in three different ways: desire, fear, and worship.

Desire

In the book of Matthew, we are given some important details concerning the birth of the Messiah:

■ *Now after Jesus was born in Bethlehem of Judea. . . (Matthew 2:1).*

When Matthew first describes the birth of Jesus in chapter 1, he does not mention the location. He only notes the response of Joseph. In chapter 2, Matthew reveals where Jesus was born: in Bethlehem of Judea. Several verses later, Matthew points out that this is the place where the prophet Micah said the Messiah would be born (Micah 5:2). Thus, it becomes clear that what was foretold concerning the birth of the Messiah in the Old Testament came to fruition in the birth of Jesus. In other words, His birth is in complete harmony with the Old Testament.

Next, Matthew tells us who the reigning king was when Jesus was born:

■ *In the days of Herod the king. . . (Matthew 2:1).*

For the original readers of the New Testament, the name of Herod the king would have immediately gotten their attention. As noted earlier, Herod had been established as king over Israel by the Roman senate. By the time Jesus was born, Herod had become very paranoid, believing that people were out to get him. Learning of the birth of the King of the Jews would have made him insane with rage.

Matthew continues with the story:

■ *Behold, wise men from the east came to Jerusalem, saying, "Where is he who has been born king of the Jews? For we saw his star when it rose and have come to worship him" (Matthew 2:1–2).*

Journey of the Magi by James Jacques Joseph Tissot (1894)

The term *Magi* (translated "wise men" here), as we find it in Matthew, does not refer to kings, as tradition often regards them, but rather to astrologers or wise men. The text also says nothing about how many there were, nor does it give them names, as many early church traditions have done. In ancient Media and Persia, the Magi were a caste of priests who interpreted the signs of the heavens as well as dreams, similar to the wise men in the book of Daniel.

The text makes it clear that these men came from the east, probably referring to Babylonia, Media, or Persia—all lands controlled by the Parthians. The reason Matthew mentions this seemingly small detail about the Magi's homeland was to point out that they came from the empire that had previously driven Herod out of Israel before he was appointed king. In other words, these men were coming from a place that posed a threat to Herod's position.

Notice what the Magi said to Herod:

■ *"Where is he who has been born king of the Jews? For we saw his star when it rose and have come to worship him" (Matthew 2:2).*

What a question to ask a man who called himself the king of the Jews! But how did the Magi know that Jesus was the King of the Jews?

Given that these men were most likely from Persia or Babylon, they would have been familiar with the book of Daniel as well as with the rest of the Jewish scriptures, because many Israelites had been exiled to Babylon when Nebuchadnezzar conquered Israel. Daniel, one of the boys captured by the Babylonians, eventually rose to become the leader of the Magi. Therefore, the Magi would have been familiar not only with the writings of Daniel but also with all the Old Testament.

One of the Old Testament books the Magi would have read was Numbers. In Numbers 24:17, reference is made to a star in an oracle given by the prophet Balaam, who was asked by the king of Moab to place a curse on the Israelites. God prevented Balaam from cursing Israel and caused him instead to pronounce many blessings on them. One of the blessings was that a star would rise out of Israel and crush the enemies of God. Many theologians believe this passage refers not only to a near-term defeat of the Moabites but also to a greater Conqueror who would arise and vanquish all the enemies of God's people.

This passage in Numbers is not the only place in the Old Testament where a star is mentioned. Numerous references are made throughout scrip-

This parchment is from an English manuscript created between 1190 and 1200. In the top frame, the Magi visit Herod. In the bottom frame, they find the baby Jesus. The original artist is unknown.

ture regarding the stars as signs from God. In Genesis 1:14, when God created the stars, He said that they were not only to light up the evening sky but also to serve as signs. So it should not be surprising that God would use a star in the sky to communicate to these astrologers that the Messiah had come.

The Magi also would have also been able to consult the prophecies of Daniel regarding the birth of the Messiah. Daniel 7–9 records many prophecies concerning the coming Messiah, as well as a detailed time line for His arrival. The wise men likely used these writings, along with the special star in the sky, to guide them to Israel and eventually to Jesus. No doubt they desired to see the fulfillment of what the scriptures foretold.

It is clear from Matthew's Gospel that the Magi did not simply want to honor the birth of an important man; instead, they came to worship Him,

The wise men visit the holy family. Original artist and date unknown.

which means they regarded Him as divine. Thus, God directed pagan religious leaders to travel hundreds of miles from the land of Herod's enemies to come and worship the Messiah He had sent to the world.

Fear

■ *When Herod the king heard this, he was troubled, and all Jerusalem with him (Matthew 2:3).*

The entire region of Israel knew the lengths that Herod would go to in order to maintain his position as king of the Jews, so when word got out that a contingent from Persia had arrived to honor another King of the Jews, Herod and all Jerusalem became troubled. Herod could hardly ignore the situation, because it may well have been that hundreds of Persian astrologers arrived at his palace with soldiers, horses, and glorious religious robes. The brilliant pageantry of their arrival would have been on grand display in Jerusalem to acknowledge the birth of a new king. What could have been more threatening for Herod? There can be no doubt that everyone wondered and feared how Herod would respond.

Thus, God arranged for the Messiah to be born right under Herod's nose (Bethlehem was only about five miles from Jerusalem), and He received the international support that a true king should receive. Let's look at how Herod responded to the arrival of this group from Persia:

■ *And assembling all the chief priests and scribes of the people, he inquired of them where the Christ was to be born (Matthew 2:4).*

Herod knew what these men were referring to, so he gathered together the chief priests and scribes to find out the location of the birth of the Messiah. It seems he knew that God had a plan and was now carrying it out. The chief priests and scribes had been put into power because of their allegiance to Herod, so they were not the most popular of religious leaders among the Jews. Nevertheless, they were very well schooled in the scriptures and were prepared to give Herod the answer:

■ They told him, "In Bethlehem of Judea, for so it is written by the prophet: 'And you, O Bethlehem, in the land of Judah, are by no means least among the rulers of Judah; for from you shall come a ruler who will shepherd my people Israel' " (Matthew 2:5–6).

> The entire region of Israel knew the lengths that Herod would go to in order to maintain his position as king of the Jews, so when word got out that a contingent from Persia had arrived to honor another King of the Jews, Herod and all Jerusalem became troubled.

Here Matthew quotes from Micah 5:2. Micah was a prophet who prophesied at about the same time as Isaiah. He lived in the southern kingdom of Judah. The king of Judah had rejected God's help, but through Micah, God told the people that the Messiah would still come and that He would come from Bethlehem. The priests and scribes in Herod's time knew this prophecy, so they were able to tell the king where the Messiah would be born.

STOP FOR A MOMENT AND CONSIDER HOW INTENSE THIS MOMENT MUST HAVE BEEN. MAGI FROM THE EAST HAVE COME TO WORSHIP THE MESSIAH; THE REIGNING KING IS AFRAID THAT THE MESSIAH HAS TRULY BEEN BORN; YET THE RELIGIOUS LEADERS MERELY ACKNOWLEDGE THE LOCATION, CHOOSING TO SHOW ALLEGIANCE TO HEROD RATHER THAN SUBMIT TO THIS MESSIAH. WHY DIDN'T ANY OF THE RELIGIOUS LEADERS COME TO WORSHIP THE MESSIAH ALONG WITH THE MAGI? WITH ALL THE SIGNS PLAYING OUT BEFORE THEM, THEY CHOSE TO DO NOTHING. THEIR ACTIONS FULFILL THE PROPHECY OF ISAIAH 53, WHICH STATES THAT THE MESSIAH WOULD BE REJECTED BY HIS OWN.

It is important to notice what Herod did next:

■ *Then Herod summoned the wise men secretly and ascertained from them what time the star had appeared. And he sent them to Bethlehem, saying, "Go and search diligently for the child, and when you have found him, bring me word, that I too may come and worship him" (Matthew 2:7–8).*

Notice that Herod summoned the Magi secretly. It is clear that he did not want anyone to know his plans. He did not want to draw any more attention to this issue. He believed the scriptures enough to know that the Messiah had been born, but he did not love God enough to submit to Him. Herod wanted to know when the star had appeared so that he could get an idea of how old the baby was. If the star had appeared when the baby king was born, discerning the time of its first appearance would help him know who to look for. Then Herod lied to the Magi, telling them to find the baby so that he could worship Him, when instead his only purpose was to eliminate any and all threats to his rule (Matthew 2:16–18). He wanted the position that God said no person could ever have. Thus, he was fighting against the will of God.

Herod was not the only person to experience fear in regard to the coming of Jesus. In a certain sense, we all experience fear, because whenever we come face-to-face with Jesus the Messiah, we have to submit to Him. We cannot rule ourselves, we cannot be in charge, and we cannot think that we can do whatever we want. We must submit to His sovereign rule. This truth threatens power-hungry leaders. Herod had come face-to-face, not just with a one-year-old baby, but with the King of kings who would ultimately dethrone him and make him a servant.

Worship

■ *After listening to the king, they went on their way. And behold, the star that they had seen when it rose went before them until it came to rest over the place where the child was. When they saw the star, they rejoiced exceedingly with great joy (Matthew 2:9–10).*

It seems that the star brought the Magi to Jerusalem, and then it disappeared so that they would stop at Herod's palace. God did this to announce to the world that the Messiah was born. This was no secret—God wanted the leaders of the world to take notice. Psalm 2 says that the Lord in heaven is going to place His King over the world, and all the kings of the earth will be humbled by Him.

Then the star reappeared, and the Magi rejoiced. In fact, they rejoiced *exceedingly*. They were overwhelmed with joy. Why were they so happy? Because the greatest desire of their hearts was about to be fulfilled. They were about to come face-to-face with the Messiah, the One for whom people had been waiting for thousands of years. The Magi followed the star until it literally rested over the house where Jesus was. Let's look at what happened next:

■ *And going into the house they saw the child with Mary his mother, and they fell down and worshiped him. Then, opening their treasures, they offered him gifts, gold and frankincense and myrrh (Matthew 2:11).*

The Magi's first response was to worship the baby King. They offered their praise and honor to this child. It is clear that these men understood that this was not just a political leader, but the One to whom all worship is due. He is the King

Gifts of the Magi

Gold, a bag of frankincense, and myrrh resin

who has come in the line of David, Immanuel, God with us (Isaiah 7:14; Matthew 1:23).

Then they opened their treasures and offered gifts to Jesus. These gifts were typically given to kings, and all of them were very rare:

- Gold: a precious metal
- Frankincense: incense that comes from a special tree
- Myrrh: a perfume used for embalming corpses

There are some who see theological significance in these gifts. Gold is given to kings, leading some to draw the conclusion that this gift recognizes the kingship of Jesus. Frankincense is burned in the presence of God, and thus it is argued that they were recognizing the divinity of Jesus. Myrrh was a perfume used in the embalming process, and thus it is thought that

Dream of Three Wise Men. This twelfth-century sculpture by Gislebertus appears on a capital from the Autun Cathedral.

by giving this gift the Magi were recognizing the significance of Jesus' eventual death.

It is not out of the question that these men would have known who Jesus was and what He came to do, and that they would have picked gifts that represented these things. Because the Magi came to worship Jesus, they knew He was worthy to be worshipped and that He was going to do things that had never been done by any human king. Because of this, many believe these gifts hold special theological significance.

After the Magi offered their worship, God protected Jesus, as well as Joseph and Mary. God did not allow the Magi to be harmed in any way. He spoke to them in a dream, warning them to stay away from Herod. God knows the hearts of all people, so even when the Magi were being manipulated, God was not. Herod could win for now—but Jesus is the eternal King!

■ *And being warned in a dream not to return to Herod, they departed to their own country by another way (Matthew 2:12).*

REFLECTIONS

This period of history progressed much like Beethoven's Ninth Symphony. It began with God appearing silent and ended with a large barrage of cannon fire at the birth of Jesus. During this period, God set the world stage for the arrival of His King. All history is moving in the direction of what God is doing in the world through Jesus, the Savior and King.

It is important to see how Jesus' birth affected the world and its leaders. Some held in their hearts a desire to see and worship Jesus, a desire so strong that they were willing to make a journey of hundreds of miles through the desert. This remains the response of some people even today.

In the hearts of others, there was fear. Why? Because Jesus is not merely a wise teacher; He is the Lord of the universe, who must be worshipped, served, and obeyed. This truth continues to lead some to fear Jesus, for it does not allow room for people to follow their own agenda, doing things their own way. Ultimately, people want to be as God, to be the center of the universe; but the Bible tells us that one day the entire world will submit to Jesus as King.

The reality is that there is no one better to rule the world and to rule our lives than Jesus. We do not know the beginning from the end. We are bound by time and only know the past and the present. It is better to place our lives and our plans in the care of the Eternal One, who ultimately decides where history is going. He is the only One who can truly rule us in the best way possible. Even when it appears that God is silent, He is not. He is always at work, bringing about His purposes for history.

A model of Herod's Temple adjacent to the "Shrine of the Book" exhibit at the Israel Museum, Jerusalem

TIME LINE
400 BC – 1 BC

| BIBLE EVENT | WORLD EVENT |

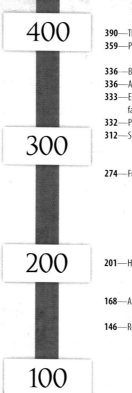

400

390—The Gauls attack Rome
359—Philip becomes king of Macedonia

336—Birth of Aristotle
336—Alexander the Great begins reign in Greece
333—End of Persian control of Palestine when it falls to Alexander
332—Ptolemy I reigns
312—Seleucus I reigns

300

274—First Punic War

The "400 Silent Years"

200

201—Hannibal defeated

168—Antiochus IV Epiphanes occupies Jerusalem

146—Rome captures Carthage

100

65—Buddhism begins to rise in China
63—Jerusalem conquered by Pompey

51—Cleopatra VII begins reign in Egypt
44—Julius Caesar assassinated
31—Caesar Augustus becomes emperor

1

5—Birth of John the Baptist
4—Birth of Jesus Christ
2—Visit of the Magi; Herod orders the death of innocent children Jesus' family flees to Egypt

4—Herod Archelaus begins rule in Judea

All dates are approximate.

CHAPTER 8

ANNO DOMINI

TURNING THE PAGE
AD 1–330

In the sixth century AD, a monk by the name of Dionysius Exiguus (Dennis the Little, a name describing his character of humility, not his physical stature) was hard at work developing a church calendar to help him accurately determine when Easter would come each year. Since the Council of Nicaea in AD 325, Easter had become an official holiday of the church; therefore, knowing the day on which it would fall was important.

In the days of the Roman Empire, years were marked by the consuls of Rome. Since many of the leaders of Rome had persecuted members of the church, however, Dionysius decided to come up with a dating system that marked time by the number of years since Christ's birth, rather than by the names of the Roman consuls. All dates after Christ's birth, as calculated by

This painting of the Council of Nicaea appears on the wall of a church in Bucharest, Romania.

> **Because Jesus is the King of kings and the Lord of lords, it is only appropriate that time itself should be marked and understood in reference to His arrival.**

Dionysius, came to be referred to as *Anno Domini* ("in the year of our Lord"), which is abbreviated as AD. All dates before Christ's birth have come to be referred to as BC, meaning "before Christ."

This new way of marking time highlights the fact that the birth of Christ was not just another religious event. Instead, it was the center of all history, the event that changed everything as we know it. Because Jesus is the King of kings and the Lord of lords, it is only appropriate that time itself should be marked and understood in reference to His arrival.

In this chapter, we turn a corner in world history. We move from 1 BC to AD 1 (there is no "year zero" in the Gregorian calendar). This last chapter will deal with the world after "the year of our Lord"—when God came to earth in the person of Jesus Christ and not only brought salvation to mankind but also changed the very way the world operates. The birth of Christ and His work on the cross affected the world not only spiritually but also politically, technologically, and socially. His coming truly is powerful. History truly is His story, and He should therefore be at the center of it all.

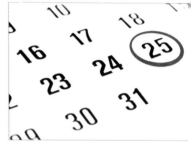

IN THIS CHAPTER, WE WILL LOOK AT HISTORY THROUGH A SINGLE LENS: THE DEVELOPMENT OF THE CHURCH. JESUS' GRAND PURPOSE IN COMING TO EARTH TO BRING ABOUT SALVATION FOR MANKIND WAS TO BRING TOGETHER PEOPLE FROM EVERY TRIBE AND EVERY NATION TO BECOME PART OF HIS BODY, THE CHURCH. THE FORMATION AND ADVANCEMENT OF THIS CHURCH, EVEN IN THE FACE OF ALL WHO SOUGHT TO DO AWAY WITH IT, ARE TRULY A REMARKABLE MIRACLE OF GOD. WE WILL LOOK AT WHAT GOD DID TO BRING HIS CHURCH INTO BEING, AND THEN WHAT HE DID TO BLESS IT AND ADVANCE IT IN THE WORLD.

THE ROMAN EMPIRE

At this point, it would be good to review a bit about the Roman Empire. Much of the world of Jesus' day was shaped by this empire, so learning more about the Romans will help us better understand the ministry of Jesus and the growth of the church.

The history of the Roman Empire from AD 1 to 300 reads like a soap opera. Rulers came and went with much drama. Like so many before them, they were leaders who had a lust for power that drove some of them mad. Let's take a closer look at a couple of leaders who had an especially significant impact on the land of Israel and the ministry of Jesus and His disciples.

Tiberius

When the Roman emperor Augustus died in AD 14, his son-in-law, Tiberius, succeeded him as emperor, because Augustus had no direct descendants who could rule. Tiberius did not have a dynamic personality, and he was a very unsure leader. After taking the throne, he moved out of Rome and sought to manage the empire from the nearby region of Capri, thereby angering the Roman senate. Tiberius's personal life was also marked by flagrant immorality.

While Tiberius was away from Rome indulging his lusts, the leader of the Praetorian Guard, a man named Lucius Aelius Sejanus, was working hard to establish himself as the next successor to the throne. In AD 23 Tiberius's son died of apparent stomach troubles, but Tiberius discovered that he had actually been murdered by Sejanus. Sejanus also conspired with Tiberius's daughter-in-law to kill Tiberius. Sejanus was arrested, tried, and found guilty of the conspiracy, and was sentenced to death. Tiberius then ordered a purge of all threats to the throne to be made throughout the empire. He sent his agents to arrest, torture, and execute countless people.

This important information forms the backdrop for Luke's description of the start of John the Baptist's ministry:

■ *In the fifteenth year of the reign of Tiberius Caesar, Pontius Pilate being governor of Judea, and Herod being tetrarch of Galilee, and his brother Philip tetrarch of the region of Ituraea and Trachonitis, and Lysanias tetrarch of Abilene. . . (Luke 3:1).*

At the time that Jesus was ministering in Galilee and Judea, Tiberius sent his agents throughout the Roman Empire to arrest and kill those he suspected of being disloyal to him. For this reason, when the Jewish leaders wanted to kill Jesus, the situation was ripe for them to

Statue of Pontius Pilate in Bom Jesus, Braga, Portugal

God arranged for Jesus to be tried and arrested during the reign of a paranoid ruler who was making all the other officials nervous and ready to bend any law to keep him happy in order to maintain peace in the land.

arrange for the Roman government to do it. The Roman officials in Israel readily recognized that Jesus had committed no crime worthy of death, yet the Jewish leaders' charge that Jesus claimed to be a king in opposition to Caesar put great political pressure on the Roman officials. If the officials failed to execute Jesus, Tiberius might see them as disloyal and have them killed. When Pilate passed Jesus to Herod, Herod opted to pass the buck and returned Jesus to Pilate. Pilate did not want to crucify Jesus either, but in order to keep the peace and avoid the wrath of Tiberius, he went ahead with it.

In the end, it was really the will of God that Jesus should be crucified, so God arranged for all the players to be ready. In any other circumstance, Jesus likely would not have been crucified in accordance with Roman law. Yet God arranged for Jesus to be tried and arrested during the reign of a paranoid ruler who was making all the other officials nervous and ready to bend any law to keep him happy in order to maintain peace in the land.

Titus

Another key Roman leader around this time was a military commander named Titus, who later became emperor as well. In AD 66 many Jews revolted against the rule of Rome and attacked the Roman garrison in Jerusalem. The

Left: *D. Titus Vespasian, Emperor of Rome.* Engraved by Aegidius Sadeler in the beginning of the seventeenth century.
Right: A close-up of the Arch of Titus. This portion depicts the sacking of the Jerusalem temple.

local governor marched troops into Jerusalem to stop the rebellion but was defeated. The rebellion quickly gained momentum, leading Rome to send its best general, Vespasian, to command the army and put down the revolt. Vespasian utilized his son Titus as a key commander in the operation.

The Romans were successful in attacking the Jewish rebels and quickly gained ground in putting down the rebellion. By AD 68 the majority of the region had been recaptured by the Romans. In December of 69 Vespasian was appointed by the Roman senate to be the new emperor, and he appointed his son Titus to finish the siege of Jerusalem and end the revolt.

When Titus finally broke down the walls of Jerusalem, he offered a peace treaty to the Jews. If they would lay down their arms, he would not fight

The Arch of Titus from the front. This archway is located in Rome.

them anymore. They rejected that treaty and continued to fight. In the end, the Romans took the city, burned it to the ground, destroyed the temple, and removed many Jews from Israel.

According to the ancient historian Tacitus, there were 600,000 people living in the city of Jerusalem. The first-century historian Josephus, who fought in this war and was taken prisoner by the Romans, reported that 97,000 people were taken prisoner, not counting those crucified or killed in battle. By the end of the third month after the war was over, 115,800 bodies were discovered. This war truly decimated the Jews who lived in the land of Israel.

Yet God was at work using these events to spread the message that the King had come and that salvation and blessing were available for everyone in the whole world.

THE BIRTH OF THE CHURCH

Now let's return to the time of Jesus, around AD 29, when His disciples were gathered on a mountain in Galilee. The resurrected Jesus stood before them, and it was there that He gave them the mission for which they would eventually give their lives:

Destruction of the Temple of Jerusalem, painted by Francesco Hayez, 1791–1882

■ *Now the eleven disciples went to Galilee, to the mountain to which Jesus had directed them. And when they saw him they worshiped him, but some doubted. And Jesus came and said to them, "All authority in heaven and on earth has been given to me. Go therefore and make disciples of all nations, baptizing them in the name of the Father and of the Son and of the Holy Spirit, teaching them to observe all that I have commanded you. And behold, I am with you always, to the end of the age"* (Matthew 28:16–20).

Stained glass window of the resurrected Christ giving the Great Commission to His disciples

Jesus had already died to suffer the punishment for mankind and had risen from the dead, signifying that God had accepted that sacrifice as sufficient for the justification of all who would believe. Now Jesus was returning to His heavenly home to prepare a place for His followers. In the meantime, His disciples were left on earth for a very important mission: they were to make disciples of all nations, baptizing them in the name of the Father, the Son, and the Holy Spirit. This mission turned out to be much bigger and much more involved than they realized at that moment, for God's plan from the beginning was to bring the message of salvation to the entire world—every nation, every tribe, every tongue—and people from around the world would be brought into the fellowship of God's Son.

After Jesus ascended to heaven and the disciples replaced Judas Iscariot with Matthias, the day of Pentecost arrived. This was one of the three most important annual feasts of the Jews, along with Passover and the Feast of Tabernacles. Passover celebrated the protection of the firstborn male children when the tenth plague came upon the Egyptians during the time of the

Exodus (Exodus 12). Pentecost, called the Feast of Harvest in the Old Testament (Exodus 23:16), celebrated the beginning of the harvest. It came fifty days after Passover, which explains the New Testament name for the feast (*pente* means "five" or "fifty" in Greek).

It is no strange coincidence that on Pentecost, the day on which Jews

from all over the world were gathered in Jerusalem celebrating the harvest, the Spirit of God descended upon the disciples, and they began to preach in the various languages of the people present. Most of these Jews were descendants of those who had been exiled from Israel long ago by the Assyrians and the Babylonians. Even when the Persians allowed the Jews to return, many did not and instead chose to continue living outside of Israel. Yet during the feasts many of these faithful Jews came to Jerusalem to worship. It was on that day that Peter stood and explained to the crowd that the Spirit of God had descended upon them as the prophet Joel had said He would (Joel 2:28–32). When Peter completed his sermon, three thousand people believed in his message, and the church of Jesus Christ was established.

Pentecost painted by Juan Bautista Maino (1569 –1649)

The emergence of the church on the world scene is very significant. Because history is the movement of the events of this world toward God's end, the creation of the church is much more than just another religious event. It is a major step forward in God's purposes for the world. Historian Philip Schaff made the following observation about the church:

> The central current and ultimate aim of universal history is the Kingdom of God established by Jesus Christ. This is the grandest and most comprehensive institution in the world, as vast as humanity and as enduring as eternity. All other institutions are made subservient to it, and in its interest the whole world is governed. It is no after-thought of God, no subsequent emendation of the plan of creation, but it is the eternal forethought, the controlling idea, the beginning, the middle, and the end of all his ways and works. The first Adam is a type of the second Adam; creation looks to redemption as the solution of its problems. Secular history, far from controlling sacred history, is controlled by it, must directly or indirectly subserve its ends, and can only be fully understood in the central light of Christian truth and the plan of salvation. The Father, who directs the history of the world, "draws to the Son," who rules the history of the church, and the Son

leads back to the Father, that "God may be all in all."

"All things," says St. Paul, "were created through Christ and unto Christ: and He is before all things, and in Him all things hold together. And He is the head of the body, the Church: who is the beginning, the firstborn from the dead, that in all things He may have the pre-eminence." Col. 1:16–18. "The Gospel," says John von Müller, summing up the final result of his lifelong studies in history, "is the fulfillment of all hopes, the perfection of all philosophy, the interpreter of all revolutions, the key of all seeming contradictions of the physical and moral worlds; it is life—it is immortality."*

Schaff clearly states that the formation of the church was a major step in God's work of bringing about His kingdom and glory. Therefore, when we study the church, we are not looking at just another religion in history. Instead, we are looking at the work of the hand of God. The church is the institution God is using to bring blessing to the whole world through Jesus Christ. The church is directly linked to the plan of God and the movement of history in the world. This is why we are going to look at history through the lens of the church in this chapter.

*Philip Schaff, *History of the Christian Church*, vol. 1 (New York: Scribner's, 1910).

Below: The fish and bread, early symbols of the church, are featured in this early mosaic.

In order to understand the church and her relationship to world history, it is important to understand the world in which the church evolved. Three main factors shaped the formation and development of the church: Judaism in Israel, Judaism around the world, and the Roman Empire.

JUDAISM IN ISRAEL

If we were to choose a single word to describe the experience of the Jews in Israel leading up to the New Testament, it would be *struggle*. Throughout the Old Testament, the Jews struggled to possess and defend their land against the many nations that fought against them. In the two centuries leading up to the formation of the church, the main struggle within Israel revolved around Hellenization. When Alexander the Great conquered the known world, he sought to establish not only his rule but also the Greek way of life. In the area of religion, the Greek way of life is founded on the principle of syncretism, which attempts to reconcile unrelated, even opposing, beliefs and practices into a new, unified whole. As noted earlier, various pagan rulers over Israel tried to force the Jews to adopt syncretistic religious beliefs, but many Jews in Israel resisted this and repeatedly struggled, even to the point of death, to maintain the purity of Judaism and their fidelity to the one true God, Yahweh.

Out of this struggle emerged a group of Jews who were very militant in preserving their faith and protecting their land. Their strong stance in de-

This Roman aqueduct in Caesarea was one of the visual reminders (and benefits) of the Roman occupation of Israel.

fense of their faith created constant conflict within the nation. Even when the Romans conquered the land and softened much of the Hellenizing that had taken place, there was still a lot of tension in the region.

Even though the Romans allowed the Jews total freedom to worship Yahweh, many Jews sought even greater independence. They wanted a theocracy—the direct rule of God over the nation—and nothing short of that would make them happy. In a theocracy, the state is governed by the mandates and standards of a particular religion and not by a secular ruler or even by representatives of the people. Many Jews did not want any king or laws other than those given to them by Yahweh. This led to constant rebellion toward the Roman government. For example, Acts 5:37 refers to a revolt that was led by a Jewish insurrectionist named Judas against the Roman leader Archelaus. Archelaus was one of Herod the Great's sons, and he ruled a portion of Israel after his father died.

Similar tensions led to many religio-political factions within Israel. One group, called the Pharisees, was known for their strict commitment to the law of God and for their strong belief in one God. The Pharisees also had high regard for the oral traditions of their predecessors, which they deemed to be essentially as authoritative as the scriptures themselves.

Another group within Israel was the Sadducees. They differed from the Pharisees in that they wanted Judaism to be centered on the temple rather than on the Law of Moses. Unlike the Pharisees, they did not hold to the oral

Jesus' first-known interaction with the Pharisees occurred when he was twelve years old. Here is Christ with the religious leaders as depicted by Alexandre Bida (1813–1895).

traditions of other religious teachers. They also had a better relationship with the Romans than the Pharisees did, because they were more open to Hellenistic and Roman ways, including policies regarding economic expansion and military service.

A third group within Israel, the Zealots, were looking for the Messiah to drive out the Romans and restore Israel to the glory of David's reign. They were willing to use military force, if necessary, to accomplish this. The Zealots were often the first group to align with any leader who would attack Rome.

The Zealots were not the only ones who were waiting for the Messiah. Every Jew longed for the Son of David to come and restore Israel. Yet each group held to a variety of opinions as to what that Messiah would be like. According to some, he would restore the Law of Moses; according to others, he would restore worship throughout the land; and still others believed that he would drive out the Romans and reestablish a Jewish kingdom.

It was in this nation filled with tension and high expectations that the church was born. When Jesus first appeared on the scene in Israel, and rumor spread that the Messiah had come, it caught the attention of every party in Israel. Yet Jesus did not fulfill the wishes of any particular party. Instead of conquering the Romans, He instructed the people to pay their taxes. He rejected the temple practices of the Sadducees and threw out their corrupt money changers. He did not uphold the law the way the Pharisees did and instead said that He Himself was the fulfillment of the Law of Moses. This put Jesus and His followers at odds with many religious leaders in Israel. Therefore, the church, too, was established in a context of suspicion and rejection by the religious establishment.

JUDAISM AROUND THE WORLD

As we've seen, by the time of the New Testament, many Jews had been scattered throughout the world as a result of the various exiles that Israel and Judah had experienced over the years. These Jewish settlements in other countries proved to be of great benefit to the church as it expanded around the world.

When the apostle Paul arrived in a city that had not yet heard the gospel, he made his first stop at the Jewish synagogue. Even though Paul was "the apostle to the Gentiles," he started his evangelistic efforts with the Jews. The synagogues ensured that at least a certain portion of the population was reading and learning about the scriptures (the Old Testament), providing an initial point of theological dialogue concerning the message about Jesus Christ.

Remains of the Synagogue Horvat in Croatia

Paul and the other apostles used the scriptures to show the people that Jesus was the fulfillment of what the prophets had announced. The synagogue also provided a meeting house for those who had embraced Jesus as the Messiah. Thus, speaking in human terms, the spread of Jews throughout the world and the establishment of synagogues in various cities are what propelled the mission of Paul to expand as it did throughout the Roman Empire.

Again, as we've seen, another important factor that allowed the gospel to spread quickly throughout the Roman world was the widespread use of the Greek language after Alexander the Great's conquests. Because the people in the Roman provinces spoke Greek and the Old Testament had already been translated into Greek, Paul was able to move from town to town and easily preach the message that Jesus was the Messiah.

THE GOSPEL AND THE ROMAN EMPIRE

The third major factor affecting the development of the church was the Roman Empire itself. The Romans did not rise to great power and sustain their empire for centuries by accident. They were very intentional in the way they governed. They maintained a strong infrastructure of roads, with civil servants to maintain the roads. In addition to enabling the Roman army to move swiftly throughout the empire, the roads fostered trade and commerce. The Romans also greatly improved the safety of shipping through various waterways. All of this made travel much more feasible and

Ancient Roman road made from cobblestones in Perge, Turkey

reliable for those with the means to do so. Therefore, as the first disciples scattered to preach the message of Jesus around the empire, they were able to travel with little restriction, and the gospel reached the four corners of the empire in a relatively short time.

THOUGH THE ROMAN EMPIRE HELPED TO ENABLE THE SPREAD OF THE GOSPEL THROUGH ITS IMPROVEMENTS IN TRAVEL, ITS POLICIES REGARDING RELIGION OFTEN LED TO NEGATIVE PRESSURES ON THE SPREAD OF THE CHURCH. LIKE THE GREEKS, WHEN THE ROMANS CONQUERED LANDS, THEY OFTEN MIXED TOGETHER THE PRACTICES OF LOCAL RELIGIONS WITH THOSE OF OTHER CONQUERED PEOPLES, IN ORDER TO HELP ASSIMILATE THE NEWLY VANQUISHED PEOPLE INTO THE ROMAN EMPIRE.

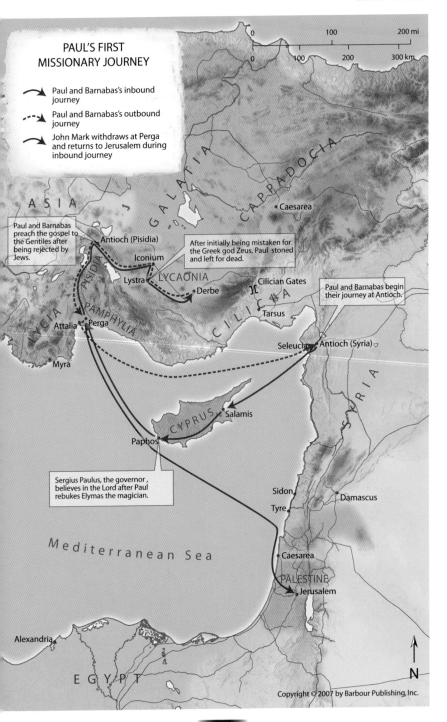

PAUL'S FIRST MISSIONARY JOURNEY

Paul and Barnabas's inbound journey

Paul and Barnabas's outbound journey

John Mark withdraws at Perga and returns to Jerusalem during inbound journey

Paul and Barnabas preach the gospel to the Gentiles after being rejected by Jews.

After initially being mistaken for the Greek god Zeus, Paul stoned and left for dead.

Paul and Barnabas begin their journey at Antioch.

Sergius Paulus, the governor, believes in the Lord after Paul rebukes Elymas the magician.

Caesarea · Antioch (Pisidia) · Iconium · Lystra · Derbe · Cilician Gates · Tarsus · Seleucia · Antioch (Syria) · Salamis · Paphos · Attalia · Perga · Myra · Sidon · Tyre · Damascus · Caesarea · Jerusalem · Alexandria

ASIA · GALATIA · CAPPADOCIA · PISIDIA · LYCAONIA · PAMPHYLIA · LYCIA · CILICIA · CYPRUS · SYRIA · PALESTINE · EGYPT

Mediterranean Sea

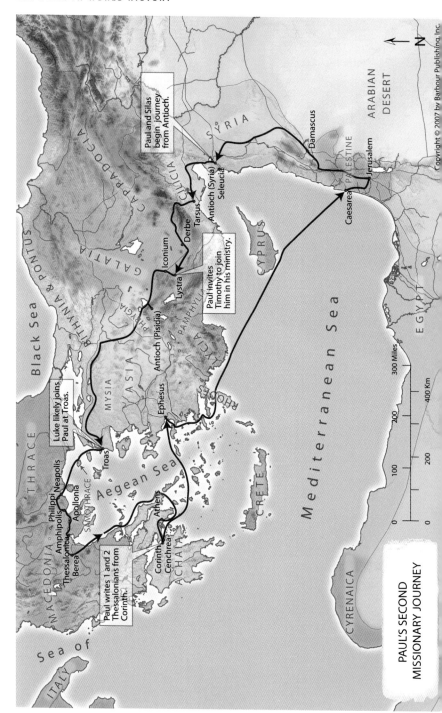

Paul and Silas begin journey from Antioch.

Paul invites Timothy to join him in his ministry.

Luke likely joins Paul at Troas.

Paul writes 1 and 2 Thessalonians from Corinth.

N

ARABIAN DESERT

Damascus

SYRIA

PALESTINE

Jerusalem

Caesarea

CYPRUS

Seleucia

Antioch (Syria)

Tarsus

CILICIA

Derbe

EGYPT

Iconium

GALATIA

Lystra

CAPPADOCIA

PHRYGIA

PAMPHYLIA

LYCIA

Antioch (Pisidia)

RHODES

ASIA

MYSIA

Ephesus

BITHYNIA & PONTUS

Black Sea

Mediterranean Sea

Troas

THRACE

Neapolis

Philippi

Amphipolis

Apollonia

SAMOTHRACE

Thessalonica

Berea

MACEDONIA

Aegean Sea

Athens

ACHAIA

Corinth

Cenchrea

CRETE

Sea of

ITALY

CYRENAICA

300 Miles

400 Km

200

200

100

0

0

Copyright © 2007 by Barbour Publishing, Inc.

PAUL'S SECOND
MISSIONARY JOURNEY

Prior to the rise of the Greeks and the Romans, people typically worshipped the god(s) of their ancestors, and they would only change their religious practices if they moved to another city where different deities were predominantly worshipped. Under the Greco-Roman system, people felt the freedom to make individual choices about the god(s) they would worship, and they could even mix together the practices of different gods. This change created a problem for the first Christians, because in addition to rejecting all gods but the God of Israel, they also refused to merge the worship of Jesus with other religions. Over time, the Christians began to be persecuted for the exclusive nature of their worship.

This huge keystone may have been used in emperor worship.

Another factor that brought about persecution for the early church was a form of worship that began to emerge in Rome in the first century: worship of the emperor. Roman authorities came to regard emperor worship as a test of loyalty to the Roman government. To refuse to burn incense before the image of the emperor became an act of treason punishable by death. Even though the early Christians submitted to the government and paid their taxes, they would not worship the emperor or treat him as a god. This put many Christians at odds with Rome. But as we will see, the persecution of the early Christians because of their beliefs did not stop the spread of the church but instead made it grow even more.

THE EXPANSION OF THE CHURCH

The message that Jesus is the Messiah and that all those who trust in Him will be saved and will become part of His body, the church, spread quickly around the world. Even the threat of death did not stop the first believers from spreading the message. God wanted this message sent to the whole world, and that is just what happened. The early growth of the church took place as follows:

For more on the expansion of the church, read the book of Acts.

- Acts 8: The believers are scattered throughout Judea and Samaria, as well as to Ethiopia.
- Acts 9: Due to persecution, the believers are scattered as far as Damascus.
- Acts 11: The believers make their way to Phoenicia, Cyprus, and Antioch.
- Acts 13: The apostle Paul brings the message of the gospel to the island of Cyprus, several cities in Asia Minor, and Greece. Later, he even helps share the gospel in Rome, where a church had already been established.

In just a few short years, the church made its way across the Roman Empire. Merchants, sailors, and military personnel that trusted in the message

of Christ began to take this message along on their travels. Christians fleeing persecution continued to share the gospel with people in new lands. As all of this was happening, the message of the church spread exponentially around the world.

As the church grew, believers began to apply the ethics of the gospel to every aspect of life. This led the church to establish hospitals, promote human rights, and care for the poor and neglected. The positive impact of the church on society began to be felt around the world.

Philippi was the location of an early church and remained so for centuries. Over a thousand years later, this cathedral was built and its remains still stand today.

THE APOSTLE PAUL

In talking about the expansion of the church, it is impossible not to mention the apostle Paul. He was a man called by God to take the gospel into places where the message had not yet been preached (see Romans 15:20). Along with spreading the gospel to new lands, Paul also wrote many letters as part of his efforts to nourish and guide the fledgling churches. Paul is probably best known for these writings, which comprise thirteen of the twenty-seven books of the New Testament:

- Romans
- 1 Corinthians
- 2 Corinthians
- Galatians
- Ephesians
- Philippians
- Colossians
- 1 Thessalonians
- 2 Thessalonians
- 1 Timothy
- 2 Timothy
- Titus
- Philemon

Stained glass window of St. Paul from St. Aidan's Cathedral, Ireland

By this time, the Jewish establishment had become critical of the Christians to a point where Christians were banned from the synagogues and regularly persecuted. Paul was born into a very devout Jewish family. He was even educated in the details of the Jewish faith by Gamaliel, one of the greatest Jewish scholars of his day. Paul (then called Saul of Tarsus) was very devoted to Judaism. One day, while on the road to Damascus to persecute Christians, he came face-to-face with the resurrected Jesus Christ. After having his eyesight temporarily taken away, Paul was made aware that what he was doing was not pleasing to God, and he began to follow Jesus as the Messiah.

Conversion of St. Paul by Luca Giordano (1632–1705)

Because he was a Roman citizen and a brilliant scholar of the scriptures, Paul was used by God to reason with the Jews, showing them that Jesus truly was the Messiah. He also preached to the Gentiles that God had prepared a way for them to be included in all the benefits promised to the Jews, including eternal life (Ephesians 3). It was this message to the Gentiles that made Paul an enemy to many of the Jews.

PERSECUTION

> The first generation of Christians. . .saw themselves in complete harmony with scripture and therefore saw themselves as true Jews.

The earliest persecution of the church came from the Jewish religious establishment. Many devout Jews saw the church as a threat to their way of life, believing that the Christians taught that there were two Gods—God the Father and God the Son. In addition, the idea that the Law of Moses was fulfilled in the work of Jesus appeared to be an attack on the scriptures. Finally, many Jews did not like the idea of including Gentiles in the promises that God had given to Israel.

The first generation of Christians did not view themselves as following a new religion or even a separate sect of Judaism. Instead, they saw themselves in complete harmony with scripture and therefore saw themselves as true Jews—those who recognized that Jesus was the fulfillment of all that the scriptures had foretold. This is the message that several of the first Christian leaders—including Stephen, Peter, and John—tried to tell those who were persecuting them; but often the leaders continued to reject Jesus as the Messiah and condemned the first Christians to death.

Nero

Eventually the persecution of the church by the Jews gave way to the persecution of the church by the Roman government. When Nero became emperor in AD 54, persecution of Christians turned from bad to worse. Nero took the throne at the age of sixteen. He was a very strong leader, but he became increasingly paranoid over time. He acted in very irrational ways and murdered many people who he believed were threats to him.

Such was the state of his leadership when on the evening of June 18, AD 64, a fire broke out in Rome. Nero was several miles away at the time, and as soon as he heard of the fire, he quickly returned and headed up the efforts to combat the blaze. The fire lasted six days and seven nights, and then flared up again from time to time for three more days.

The Roman citizens wanted the ones responsible for the fire punished, though many began to suspect that Nero himself had started the fire to clear space for a new palace and to rebuild Rome in a way that brought him glory. Over time, stories began to circulate regarding Nero's erratic behavior during the fire that did not paint him in a good light. Some stories were true, while others were just rumors. As the stories began to spread, however, Nero

The Christian Martyrs' Last Prayer
by Jean-Léon Gérôme (1824–1904)

needed to find a scapegoat to blame. He chose the Christians. He placed the full responsibility for the fire upon the followers of Christ and began a systematic attack against all Christians.

Nero devised the cruelest of tortures for the Christians—such as wrapping them in the skins of wild animals and throwing them into a pack of wild dogs to be eaten alive. He burned Christians alive—and occasionally burned them at night to provide light in his courtyard. It was during this attack

against the church that the apostles Paul and Peter were executed. Peter was crucified, and tradition states that he asked to be crucified upside down because he felt unworthy to die in the same manner as Jesus. Paul was beheaded, which was one of the acceptable means of executing a Roman citizen.

For the next several hundred years, the church continued to face persecution, though the nature of the persecution changed over time. The clearest description of the persecution of the church in the second century comes from the correspondence between the governor of Bithynia and the emperor of Rome.

In AD 111 a man named Pliny was appointed governor of Bithynia in the northern part of Asia Minor (modern-day Turkey). Much of

Beheading of St. Paul

Bithynia had converted to Christianity by this time, thus the pagan temples were emptying out and businesses around the temples were suffering. It was against the law to be a Christian, so Pliny rounded up the Christians and ordered them to recant. When they refused, he tortured or killed them.

Eventually Pliny wrote a letter to Emperor Trajan, asking for advice on handling the Christians. Trajan responded by instructing Pliny not to round

them up. But Trajan said that if an accusation was made against a Christian and the Christian appeared in court, the magistrate was to command the Christian to renounce Jesus. If the person refused, then he or she would be charged with the crime of rebellion. Tertullian, one of the early Christian leaders, wrote extensively on this law.

This type of systematic persecution lasted until the reign of Marcus Aurelius in AD 161. He was a brilliant thinker and was probably one of the smartest emperors in the history of the Roman Empire. He left behind a collection of meditations that is considered a literary masterpiece. During his reign, however, the empire suffered a string of invasions, constant floods, horrible epidemics, and other disasters. The religious

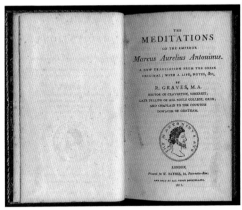

Title page of an 1811 edition of *Meditations* by Marcus Aurelius Antoninus, translated by R. Graves

men of his day blamed the Christians for angering the gods by not sacrificing to them, and Aurelius agreed with them. Thus, Christians were charged with the crime of atheism, because they did not believe in the gods of the empire.

By the end of the second century, the Roman Empire was experiencing numerous conflicts from civil war inside the empire and from barbarian attacks from outside. These conflicts helped to lessen the persecution against the church, as the empire needed to focus its attention on these other threats.

By the beginning of the third century, however, the church faced even greater persecution than ever before. The emperor Septimius Severus put an end to the civil wars and stopped the attacks of the barbarians. In order to create a stronger united front against Rome's enemies, he mandated that people could worship their own god(s) as long as their chief allegiance was to the sun god. When the Christians refused to submit to this syncretistic approach to religion, they were heavily persecuted, and this lasted until the rule of Constantine in the fourth century. After Constantine began to follow Christ, he not only stopped the persecution but favored Christianity, which later became the official religion of the empire.

Left: Emperor Trajan. Inset: This kiosk is a popular tourist attraction in northern Egypt and is believed to have been built by Trajan.

CONSTANTINE

AFRICA AND THE CHURCH

In our survey of world history, one of the places we have not looked at very closely is Africa. We are now going to examine the contributions that Africa has made to sacred and redemptive history, especially during the era of the church. In fact, it is almost impossible to understand the movement of God and the advancement of the church without looking at the continent of Africa.

When we think about the development of early Christian thought, most would not consider the importance of Africa. Yet it is true that the seedbed of many of the theological thoughts and ideas that Christians hold dear today have their roots on the African continent.

In 2007 Thomas Oden wrote a wonderful book entitled *How Africa Shaped the Christian Mind*. Oden's thesis is that, during the first few centuries of the church, African Christians were the primary figures who helped formulate the doctrine and catechism and defend the faith from heresy. Throughout its history, the church has drawn many of its theological ideas from the works of those who lived in Africa.

Oden notes seven contributions to the church around the world that were born out of Africa:

- The idea of a university education
- The creation of an exegetical system for studying the Bible
- The development of some of the first dogmas of the church
- The development of early Christian ecumenical work
- The development of the disciplines of walking with God
- The development of a Christian "philosophy" of life
- The development of a Christian apologetic in defending the faith

The early theologians who devised these contributions came primarily from North Africa. From AD 1 to the early 400s, this area of the world was under the rule of the Roman Empire. This led to many advantages for life in North Africa, such as the

Church of St. Augustine in Annaba

protection and economic development that the Roman Empire fostered in all its territories. This had a huge impact on the quality of life for those in this region.

Several other factors also helped foster the environment in which Christian thought took shape on the African continent. Three of these, in particular, are especially important.

The School of Alexandria

When Alexander the Great conquered Egypt, he established the city of Alexandria in the Nile Delta on the shores of the Mediterranean Sea. In the years that followed, the Greek rulers of Egypt developed the city into a great center of learning. One unique aspect of their approach to learning was the blending of Greek and Near Eastern ideas.

The city developed a reputation for outstanding scholarly work, much of which was collected in the great library that was built there during this time. Because Alexandria was a coastal city, the scribes at the library could easily interact with people from all over the world, and the library grew as the scribes copied works of literature brought by sailors to Alexandria's shores. All

The modern-day Library of Alexandria

of this fueled learning in the city, which became a renowned source of poetry, geography, history, mathematics, astronomy, and medicine.

In addition to the library, Alexandria established a very impressive museum. When we think of a museum today, we usually think of it as a place where interesting works of art or historical artifacts are stored for the public to view. Originally, however, museums were more like think tanks or research centers. They were places where people would go to muse, discuss, and research.

When the Romans took over Egypt from the Greeks, they inherited this extensive learning system. They did not stop what was happening in Alexandria, and this allowed the city to remain a world-class center of learning.

When the gospel made its way into North Africa, those who had been exposed to this system of learning and collecting knowledge became many of the sharpest Christian thinkers in the world. Therefore, when the church faced persecution, heresy, and challenges to its way of worship, it was from the school of Alexandria that some of the best minds in the world responded.

THE MEN WHO SPOKE UP AT THIS TIME WERE CALLED THE APOSTOLIC FATHERS. THIS NAME REFERS TO THE FIRST GROUP OF THEOLOGIANS WHO TRANSITIONED THE CHURCH FROM THE TIME OF THE APOSTLES (WHO WERE DIRECT EYEWITNESSES TO JESUS AND HIS EARTHLY MINISTRY) TO THE NEXT GENERATION, WHO LIVED AND MINISTERED AFTER THE TIME OF THE APOSTLES. THESE EARLY LEADERS WERE APOLOGISTS, DEFENDERS OF ORTHODOXY, AND DEVELOPERS OF DOCTRINE. THEY BROUGHT TO THE WORLD SOME OF THE BEST DEFENSES OF THE FAITH AND BECAME THE ONES WHO HELPED TO CRYSTALLIZE OUR UNDERSTANDING OF THE CHURCH, THE GOSPEL, AND THE MISSION OF THE CHURCH. THEY ALSO DEVELOPED SOME OF THE MOST IMPORTANT DOCTRINAL STATEMENTS, WHICH ARE STILL USED TODAY IN DEFENDING AND DESCRIBING THE FAITH.

THESE EARLY LEADERS CAME FROM MANY DIFFERENT PLACES THROUGHOUT THE ROMAN EMPIRE, BUT THOSE WHO CAME FROM EGYPT WERE AMONG THE MOST INFLUENTIAL THINKERS, BECAUSE THEY HAD BEEN EXPOSED TO SOME OF THE BEST EDUCATION AVAILABLE ON THE EARTH AT THAT TIME.

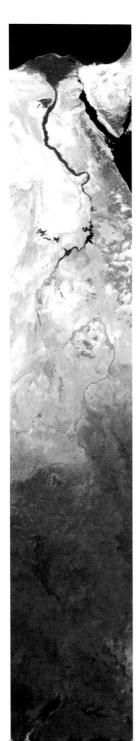

The Rivers of Africa

A second factor in North Africa that greatly affected the growth of the church was the two main rivers found in this part of the continent. In North Africa, as elsewhere, life developed around the major waterways: chiefly, the Nile and the Bagradas Rivers. The Bagradas flows from modern-day Algeria to Tunisia. The Nile flows through the Sudan into Egypt. Along these rivers, civilizations emerged, which also fostered commerce. As people along these rivers traded goods, a common trade language developed to allow them to communicate more easily. For example, along the Nile River a common language called Nilotic developed. These common trade languages became the vehicle for grassroots Christianity to spread within these regions.

Along both the Nile and the Bagradas, many great thinkers emerged to defend the faith and help to interpret the teaching of the apostles for later generations. Among them were such great men as Tertullian, Cyprian, Arnobius, Optatus, and Augustine of Hippo. The thoughts and ideas of these men have shaped the world for thousands of years.

The Unity of the Church

There is a third factor that helped to shape the church in significant ways: the unity of the African church. When the church was founded in Alexandria, a bishop was appointed as a means of fostering unity within the whole of the continent. The church in Egypt is traditionally believed to have been founded by Mark, who then became bishop over all the churches on the continent of Africa.

The unity of the North African church under one bishop allowed for a greater flow of thoughts and ideas among the people who lived along the Nile and the Bagradas Rivers. This unity of thought then contributed to the advancement of North African theology in the world. The impact this had on the world is still felt today. For example, Augustine of Hippo's works have influenced theologians of every generation since, and his masterpiece, *The City of God*, is considered one of the most influential works ever written by a theologian, outside of the Bible itself.

If we look at the great school of learning in Alexandria, the great unity around the Nile and Bagradas Rivers, and even the ecumenism of the church in North Africa, it becomes clear how greatly African Christianity affected the world. Coming from this region are the exegetical works of Origen, the defense of Christianity by Tertullian, and the monumental works of the great theologian Augustine. The writings of these men addressed key issues such as sin, the nature of Jesus Christ, the doctrine of the Holy Spirit, the understanding of the kingdom of man and the kingdom of God, the doctrine of justification, and the canon of scripture. They also led to other works that further examined these issues. Truly we stand on the shoulders of the theologians who came from Africa.

Tertullian's *Apologeticus*

REFLECTIONS

At the beginning of this chapter, we noted that time came to be marked by the birth of Jesus. Anno Domini, or "the year of our Lord," is a very apt description of history after the birth of Jesus. The incarnation of Jesus helps make sense of history. History is moving toward God's ends; and as He has shown us, His ends are moving toward the reign of His Son over all. When Jesus came into the world, we saw not only God, but God interacting with the world. We saw our sin and our propensity to walk away from God.

And we saw how God dealt with that sin—by punishing Jesus instead of us. When we embrace the forgiveness of God through Jesus Christ, we embrace not only the salvation of our souls but the understanding that God is moving history to His ends and that history will ultimately benefit His children.

The future is already written, the end is already known, and those who have trusted in the King of kings have the great hope of knowing that when the last chapter of the history of the world is recorded, they will be in heaven with God.

The study of history should encourage the children of God to find peace and hope that God is in control and that there is nothing to fear.

The study of history should encourage the children of God to find peace and hope that God is in control and that there is nothing to fear. This is why we can say with Paul:

■ *I consider that the sufferings of this present time are not worth comparing with the glory that is to be revealed to us. For the creation waits with eager longing for the revealing of the sons of God. For the creation was subjected to futility, not willingly, but because of him who subjected it, in hope that the creation itself will be set free from its bondage to corruption and obtain the freedom of the glory of the children of God. For we know that the whole creation has been groaning together in the pains of childbirth until now. And not only the creation, but we ourselves, who have the firstfruits of the Spirit, groan inwardly as we wait eagerly for adoption as sons, the redemption of our bodies. For in this hope we were saved. Now hope that is seen is not hope. For who hopes for what he sees? But if we hope for what we do not see, we wait for it with patience* (Romans 8:18–25).

Come quickly, Lord Jesus; come quickly!

TIME LINE
AD 1 – AD 100

BIBLE EVENT | WORLD EVENT

AD 1

8—Jesus amazes the religious leaders when He visits the temple as a child

14—Tiberius becomes emperor of Rome

25

26—John baptizes Jesus
30—Jesus crucified and raised from the dead
32—Stephen, the deacon, is martyred
37—Paul is converted
44—James is martyred
45—James written
47—Paul begins first missionary journey
49—Council of Jerusalem; Paul begins second missionary journey; Galatians written
51—1 & 2 Thessalonians written
52—Paul begins third missionary journey
55—1 & 2 Corinthians written
57—Romans written
60—Ephesians, Philippians, Colossians, Philemon written
63—Titus written
65—1 Peter, 1 Timothy written
67—2 Timothy, Hebrews, 2 Peter written
68—Peter and Paul both martyred
70—Jude written?
85—John exiled to Patmos; 1, 2, 3 John written
90—Revelation written

26—Pontius Pilate becomes governor of Judea

37—Caligula becomes emperor of Rome; birth of Josephus
43—Claudius conquers portions of Britain

50

54—Nero becomes emperor of Rome

64—Rome burns; Nero blames the Christians
66—The Jews rebel against Rome
70—Titus sacks Israel; temple destroyed

75

79—Pompeii destroyed by Mt. Vesuvius
81—Domitian becomes emperor of Rome

All four Gospels were written in the first century. Their exact dates are difficult to determine.

90—Domitian persecutes the Christians

100

All dates are approximate.

ACKNOWLEDGMENTS

The Bible is the Word of God given to us. God has spoken, and we can read what He has said. For this reason man does not live by bread alone but by every word that comes from the mouth of God (Deuteronomy 8:3). I love the Bible, and I want everyone to love it as much as I do. That is the passion that drives this book. It is my deepest desire that this book would help you read the Bible with a better understanding of how the events of scripture fit within the progress of history. It is not my heart to present stale history but to declare the glory of the God of all history by observing His hand in the movements of history. My prayer is that you would have a bigger view of God after reading this book and that the pages of scripture would come alive as you see the environment in which they were recorded.

I am indebted to many people who have taught me and informed my own thinking concerning the history of the world. As you read this book, you will observe the imprint of many scholars who have paved the way to understanding the events of history. The works of these scholars season almost every page of this book. Any strengths in this book belong to them; the weaknesses are mine alone.

Below is a list of some of the seminal works that provided the undergirding for this book. I would encourage you to become familiar with these works, for they are worth the investment of time to read.

- Bauer, Susan Wise. *The History of the Ancient World: From the Earliest Accounts to the Fall of Rome*. New York: W. W. Norton & Company, 2007.
- Boice, James Montgomery. *Foundations of the Christian Faith: A Comprehensive and Readable Theology*. Rev. ed. Downers Grove, IL: InterVarsity Press, 1986.

- Josephus, Flavius. *The Works of Josephus.*
- Konstam, Angus. *Ancient World Commanders: From the Trojan War to the Fall of Rome.* Metro Books, 2008.
- Oden, Thomas C. *How Africa Shaped the Christian Mind: Rediscovering the African Seedbed of Western Christianity.* Downers Grove, IL: Inter Varsity Press, 2007.
- Schaff, Philip. *History of the Christian Church.* 3rd ed. 8 vols. Peabody, MA: Hendrickson Publishers, 2006.
- Tacitus, Cornelius. *The Annals of Imperial Rome.*
- Wells, H. G. *The Outline of History: The Whole History of Man.* 2 vols. Garden City, NY: Garden City Books, 1949.

May God truly bless you as you read this book, and may the same Spirit who revealed and inspired the scriptures illuminate them in your mind and heart.

Dr. Stephen Leston
Soli Deo Gloria

TOPIC INDEX

ART CREDITS